LIVING FREE

H.A. WILLIAMS

continuum

Continuum UK
The Tower Building
11 York Road
London SE1 7NX

Continuum US
80 Maiden Lane
Suite 704
New York, NY 10038

www.continuumbooks.com

First published 2006

British Library Cataloguing-in-Publication Data
A catalogue record for this book is available from the British Library.

ISBN 0–8264–9469–2

Typeset by BookEns Ltd., Royston, Herts.
Printed and bound by Cromwell Press, Trowbridge, Wiltshire.

CONTENTS

When I arrived at Trinity College, Cambridge in 1966, almost straight from school and without the benefit of today's gap year, the then Dean of Trinity, The Reverend Harry Williams, was a memorable figure amongst what seemed to be a veritable galaxy of extraordinarily talented and eccentric individuals. In those days, thank God, people weren't forced to retire at seventy, so the College was populated by characters whose inter-action with each other – or not – was worthy of the best novels in the English Canon. Some of my tutors were towering figures in the world of his-tory, with whom a tutorial could prove an alarm-ing experience when confronted by their views on, for instance, my Great Great Great Grandmother, Queen Victoria, and the require-ment to argue your case in front of them after writing a throroughly indifferent essay.

In this particular grove of Academe, Harry Williams proved to be a star; a man of intense

humanity and warmth whose humour and origi-
nality created an aura of approachability. His sermons in Trinity College Chapel, Great St Mary's
and elsewhere – some of which I was privileged
enough to attend when there was virtually standing room only – were an extension of this
approachability. His courageous willingness to
open up his inner soul and being and to speak
from the heart about his own experience of
the vicissitudes, complications and agonies of life
struck a powerful and immediate chord with
huge numbers of undergraduates. His sermons
were indeed memorable and remain an indelible
and essential image of my time at Cambridge. At
that stage in my life I had no idea of the importance of his role as a leading Anglican theologian
– it was his irrepressible approachability that I
recall which was exemplified by the wonderful
parties he gave in his rooms for us undergraduates. The most memorable were those attended
by his old friend, John Betjeman, at whose feet it
was pure joy to sit.

Others can write with far greater perception and
knowledge than I can about Harry Williams'
legacy; I can only pay an inadequate tribute to his
all-pervading humanity and sensitivity which

inspired so many of those of us who were lucky enough to have coincided with his time at Trinity and who came under his spell. After he left Trinity he wrote a letter to me each Christmas for the rest of his life – letters that I treasure for their wisdom and compassion. Towards the end of his life I managed to visit Harry in his cell at Mirfield, surrounded by books and increasingly immobile. He told me not to come and visit him again as his life was coming to an end.

His essence may have evaporated, but his heartening and profoundly sympathetic insight into our humanity and into the relationship between God and Man – what he called "our identity with Life Universal, with God" will live on through the power and presence of his words and through the affectionate memories of his old undergraduates.

ONE

Living Free

If I were clever enough to write a play, I should like to include a character who from time to time evaporated into the atmosphere. He might, for instance, be in a pub and slowly become no more than the smell of beer or whisky. He might next be in the university library and become no more than the pile of books in front of him. He could then be an advertisement for the smart life, somebody who storms the establishment and becomes one of its favourite protégés, thus evaporating into an executive suit (I believe that's what it's called). Or, alternatively, he could be the concentrated essence of rebellion for its own sake and become a pair of filthy, badly fitting jeans. It is probable that at one point he would become a bed – its width I would rather leave to your imagination. And then, of course, he could become the dim religious light of a church, smelling of damp and hassocks and the smoke of extinguished candles.

The play, admittedly, would present rather severe problems of production. How could an actor of flesh and blood slowly evaporate into an atmosphere or become no more than part of the scenery? Even with the most modern stage equipment the transformation would look contrived, not to say absurd.

For that is the trouble with people. They won't become no more than part of the scenery. I said 'the *trouble* with people', but that was only from the playwright's and producer's point of view. People's solidity, their incapacity to be merged completely with their surroundings, is in fact their asset of supreme value. It is what makes you you and me me. In some way or other, to some degree or other, we can't help being our independent selves, in the last resort irreducible to anything else.

It is this final independence of our personal identity which makes us free to travel. Because in the last resort you are you and I am me, we needn't stay where we are, breathing in some particular atmosphere amid some particular arrangement of scenery. We can travel elsewhere. We are always free to travel elsewhere.

Sometimes it is in a negative way that we sense our freedom to travel. That happens when we feel stuck. We know intuitively for certain that we are not just part of the atmosphere or scenery, yet we seem to be chained to it. We seem stuck in a place where we don't want to be. When, for instance, I first came to university, it was fun trying myself out as a thinking-machine, and the exercise brought me some very genuine riches of personality. But now I sense that it is not enough. I want to be more than the machine, but I seem stuck to it. Why, only yesterday I found myself trying to work out Betty as if she were a complicated differential equation. And then, as if that were not enough, I found myself subjecting the Boat Club to sociological analysis. And Tom, who is less keen on my company than he used to be – Tom, I have neatly docketed as a schizoid. (That is the best of psychology as no more than an intellectual discipline. You can always make it work in your own favour and to other people's disadvantage.) Yet I get glimpses of the absurdity of being thus stuck to my own thinking-machine.

Or I may feel stuck to my social persona. I have distributed a picture of myself as a certain sort of person: clubbable, witty, sensible, superior, sceptical, irreverent, devout, strict, pious – whatever it may be, and I'm beginning to find it rather a strain living up to the picture. And it is all the more difficult because in a way I truly am what my picture portrays. But I am also many other things as well, and it is keeping these many other things under the counter which is a strain. I feel I must go on playing the role I have chosen:

> With 'No Admittance' painted on
>   my heart
> I go abroad and play my public part.
>   (Basil Dowling)

Or I may be stuck as a lovelorn loon. I am dying of my passion for Betty. It is Betty, isn't it? Well, last year actually it was Sally; and the year before that it was Jenny. But yes, this year it is Betty. (Please don't think I have no experience of the terrible pain which comes from the love which is not returned. It is certainly no joking matter, however funny outsiders find it.) Anyhow, here I am, tied to a desperate feeling I can't shake off.

Then there are all the traditions of belief and conduct with which I was brought up. As a rational being I have discarded many of them, but they still cling to me, sometimes making me feel wretchedly guilty. I remember the oldest of my aunts – she was born in 1867 – telling me that she was brought up to regard novel-reading on Sunday as extremely wicked. She realized it wasn't, and, at 20, after she got married, she indulged in the practice with her husband's support. But, she said, it made her feel awful, especially as the third time she did it there was a terrific thunderstorm. I suspect that most of us suffer from ingrained prohibitions of this kind, however much reason bids us discard them. Some of them, of course, will be reasonable, like not kicking a man when he's down. But that is no problem.

In general, we all at times feel stuck in the past, as though now we were the prisoners of what we have been. That is obviously true with regard to our failure. We couldn't do it last time and so we feel we shan't be able to do it the next time round. But success, too, builds its own prison walls, because we feel the need, and indeed the necessity, of living up to our success. We don't want to be the man who once had a brilliant future. So the success, as well as liberating us, consigns us to a rut of nervous apprehension in which we get stuck fast.

This sense of being stuck I have called the negative way of sensing our freedom to travel. It is very important that we should realize how much of the positive there is in this negative. If we had been completely absorbed by the atmosphere and scenery we should be completely unaware of

7

being stuck. That we do feel stuck is an indication of our freedom. In the face of everything which surrounds and confines us we are asserting our inalienable identity, saying, 'I am me. I am not the scene to which I am tied. I am not the persona I appear to be. I am a person.' And the birthright of every person is freedom – freedom to travel out from where I am to what is more fulfilling and worthwhile. So we mustn't be taken in by the discomfort and unease of feeling we are stuck, nor allow its depressing effects to overwhelm us. For in fact what we are sensing is the first vital breath of our liberation. It is a pity that the phrase 'divine discontent' has become a cliché, because it tellingly expresses the method life uses to call us forth from captivity to what we have been to the glorious liberty of our full true selves. As Emerson wrote: 'People wish to be settled; only as far as they are unsettled is there any hope for them?'[1] Our divine discontent is the awakening of our awareness that we are free to travel.

[1] Ralph Waldo Emerson, *The Complete Prose Works* (London: Ward Lock, 1909), p. 80.

Our journey will be a voyage of discovery, the
slow discovery (though probably by fits and
starts) of what human life and the world are ultimately about and how we fit in to the general
scheme of things. For only by discovering our
true environment (as opposed to stage scenery)
can we become fully and rewardingly ourselves.
So if our quest is for self-fulfilment (which it is),
that can be no selfish search which disregards the
needs and rights of others. It is obvious that all of
us are deeply interrelated, so that we can be truly
ourselves only to the degree in which everybody
else has the space and opportunity to be fully
themselves. Selfishness leads to sterility, not to
fulfilment. It was this social dimensions of personal fulfilment which led Jesus to the discovery
of the paradox which cost him everything:
'Whoever would save his life shall lose it and
whoever loses his life shall save it' (Lk. 17.33).

Of Jesus dying in agony upon the cross for the
love of others, Albert Schweitzer wrote that here
we see life-affirmation and world-affirmation at
their strongest and highest. If anybody says that
self-fulfilment is a selfish goal, he is misusing the
word fulfilment, disregarding the fact that I can
become myself only among others. And perhaps

our concern can't stop at the human race. How far, for instance, can we share Blake's angry assertion: 'A robin redbreast in a cage / Puts all Heaven in a rage'? Certainly, we are aware today of the evils of pollution and of how we are raping the earth in a fit of mad greed for its natural resources. Must it not be in terms of the world as a whole that we must seek personal fulfilment?

Our journey, as we have seen, will be the discovery and appropriation of our true selves. But we shall not travel along a motorway which goes more or less in a straight line direct to its destination. We shall travel like one of those country buses I have come to know so well in the West Riding, which takes you to Leeds by threading its way in and out of endless small towns and villages. To change the image slightly, travelling in all sorts of zig-zags, sometimes coming back almost to the place you started from, you will pick up pieces of your true self on the way, a bit here, and a bit there, and a bit in the other place. In your studies, you will pick up quite a lot of yourself, discarding old and inadequate mental attitudes for new and better ones. You will become a person who can see further than you did, and more clearly. In your social life you will discover things about yourself by bumping up against other people, and the result will be the realization that you are a bigger person than you thought and also a smaller one, a nicer person and also a nastier one. But, perhaps more than anything, it is by means of your deeply felt love, in the sheer bliss and agony of it, whether it be for somebody of the opposite sex or for somebody of your own – it is by means of your most deeply felt love that you will find and gather up all sorts of things which belong to you – joy, wonder, delight, sorrow, disappointment, pain, self-giving, constancy, sensitivity to another's needs, your power both to act, to take the initiative, and to suffer.

The ins and outs of the journey will in detail be different for each of us. And often, perhaps most of the time, we shan't be very aware that we *are* travelling, if we are aware of it at all. It may just seem one thing after another. But we shall be none the less slowly threading our way to our full stature as human persons. And the more mistakes we make, the things we subsequently regret having done or failed to do, even what we have done wrong, what clerics call our sins, can advance us on our journey. The Prodigal Son, after all, really discovered his home only by leaving it awhile for the Far Country – a very roundabout way no doubt to his final destination, but a successful one in the end. The great Australian novelist Patrick White wrote: 'I feel that the moral flaws in myself are more than anything my creative source.'[2] Could Shakespeare have written *Othello* if he had known nothing of jealousy?

Our freedom to travel is our freedom to travel onwards in a far from straight line from the half- or quarter-people we are towards the mature richness which we all have it in us to attain. That richness cannot be described because it takes a unique form in every person since every person is unique. So there can be no neatly formulated account of it. We come across it in some of the people we know and we can read about it in a multitude of biographies. By such people and books we are encouraged and inspired. But we can also be misled. For it is our own richness that we have to discover and appropriate, and it will not be identical with that of our heros. Maturity does not consist of being a copycat, even a copy-

[2] Patrick White, quoted in Peter Beatson, *The Eye and the Mandala* (London: Paul Elek, 1976).

cat of perfection. For it is only externals which can be copied, not the inner essence of a person. I remember an undergraduate once telling me that he wanted above everything to be like Professor Mackinnon sitting at his desk littered with books. When I told him that he could begin to make his dreams come true by reading some books, he went away sorrowful.

Travelling onwards (I am sorry, but we can't avoid these spatial metaphors, even if repeated often they begin to sound ridiculous) – travelling onwards is also the way in which we travel inwards. That is what I meant when I said that in the course of our zig-zag journey we pick up bits and pieces of our true selves. We begin to discover who and what we really are. Our freedom to travel is most importantly the freedom to travel inwards to our own depths. Inwards and downwards is the most vital of all the directions we go. That is not an alternative journey to the journey onwards through the zig-zag. It is the same journey better understood and more fully appreciated.

What do we find as we travel inwards? We find a great variety of things – some of them valuable, some of them trash, some of them destructive – destructive because so far we have ignored them and thus withheld from them the opportunity to be creative. (If, for instance, you haven't given your mind the opportunity of kicking the hell out of a book and making it deliver its mental goods, you will probably want to kick the hell out of your neighbour.) But that is by the way. Travelling inwards we find this jumble of things – good, bad, useful, obsolescent, some things of beauty and some very ugly things. But we can travel inwards and downwards beyond this extraordinary jumble. We can travel to the place where every now and then we can catch a glimpse, generally rather a fleeting glimpse, of our final and ultimate identity, of who and what we most really and most fully are. And here we see that, although we are still individual people, unique and unrepeatable, that is not the whole truth about us, nor anything like it. We discover that we are also the recipients and conductors of one single Life which permeates the whole expanding universe and makes it what it is. We discover that we are not only the recipients of that one single Life which informs all things, but that we are also its limbs, its carriers, its agents, the means whereby that one Life finds expression and activates itself – does things. We discover our final identity as people who are securely their individual selves because they are completely caught up in the one pervading Life that flows through all that is. So close and so intimate is our relationship with that all-pervading Life, so real is the presence and power of that Life within us, so unmistakably do we recognize it as what we ourselves most truly and fully are, that the only word we can use to describe our personal relation to this one Life is the word 'identity', inadequate and misleading though that word can be. Perhaps we could put it thus: I am me; but the me I am is more than my individual ego. The me I am is Life universal and eternal. As Jesus said – and it is true of all of us – 'I and the Father are One.' Our freedom to travel culminates in our travelling inwards to that great discovery of our oneness with Life universal. And as a consequence of our discovery, without any self-consciousness or artificial effort we can be fully and forcefully our own individual and unique selves as Jesus was, because he knew, as we can know, that God and man are one.

I said that to talk of our identity with Life Universal, with God, was the only way we could put it, inadequate (and hence misleading) though the word 'identity' could be. Perhaps instead of the language of discourse we should use the language of music. The harmony of a chord is one thing, one identity. But by definition a chord is composed of a number of notes. So God and man (and I would add the world too) constitute a chord. But not one chord only. For static music is a contradiction in terms. One chord succeeds another majestic rhythm as together God, man and the world exercise that final freedom to travel which is the risk and the adventure of love.

TWO

Change

In thinking about institutional change in accordance with the Gospel, I happened to be reading J.P. Whelan's book on von Hügel.[1] It provided an example of how hasty and rash we can be in thinking we have discovered the relevance of the Gospel to a contemporary situation. During the First World War, von Hügel served on a committee calling itself the Religion and the Army Committee. It consisted of 30 members drawn from all the main Christian denominations in England, and its function was to see how the Gospel could be made relevant to the troops. One of its meetings was held six or seven weeks after the Armistice was signed in 1918. At the meeting 27 out of the 30 members of the committee were certain that new light had indeed broken forth out of God's Holy Word, that the Gospel fitted the contemporary situation like a glove. All the references in the New Testament to be Second Coming of Christ, the Messianic Age, the Millennium and so forth were seen to be applicable to the peace which had now been signed. This, not in a fundamentalist and *Old Moore's* sort of way, but in a more general and

[1] J.P. Whelan, *The Spiritual Doctrine of Friedrich von Hügel* (London: Collins, 1971).

scholarly sense. The New Testament spoke of a Golden Age succeeding a time of great travail. The war had been a time of travail. The peace now achieved could be understood as Christ's return at last to earth to inaugurate a Golden Age, what a few months later Lloyd George was to put into secular terms by promising the electorate a land fit for heroes to live in. Von Hügel went away from the meeting in a state of deep distress. How, he asked himself, how could these devout, educated, experienced Christians be so utterly blind to the true meaning of the Gospel? Well, their eyes were to be opened in a year or so by the actual march of events. But the incident is worth remembering as a caution against being too glib in our understanding of what 'in accordance with the Gospel' means. The Gospel is too elusive (because it is too real), too elusive to be neatly and satisfactorily pinned down. And here I would like to add another warning from somebody who wrote during the Second World War – Simone Weil:

> we do not obtain the most precious gifts
> by going in search of them but by
> waiting for them. Man cannot discover
> them by his own powers and if he sets

out to seek for them he will find in their
place counterfeits of which he will be
unable to discern the falsity.[2]

So let me begin by asking a question: how far and
in what ways has the Gospel to do with our need
to wait, to wait upon the Lord expectantly in faith
and so with discarding the urge to rush to hasty
and superficial conclusions. It is natural for us to
want to know exactly where we are and exactly
what is happening. But perhaps in the providence
of God it is our calling to be left in the dark, not
of course totally in the dark but to a great extent
in the dark – in the sense of the Johannine
prologue 'the light shines in the darkness and
the darkness has not overcome it'. I recall here
William Temple's exposition of the beams from a
lighthouse on a dark night: beams which certainly do not illuminate the coastline as a whole, but
which are enough for a passing ship. We shall
always want to ask, 'Lord wilt thou, or wilt thou
not at this time, restore the kingdom to Israel?'
But perhaps this is a question we should leave to
the journalists to earn their bread and butter by

[2] Simone Weil, *Waiting on God* (London: Collins/
Fontana, 1959).

attempting, in all honesty and integrity, to answer. Perhaps we should be more concerned with the Lord's own answer: 'It is not for you to know the times or the seasons which the Father has left in his own authority, but wait, and you shall be clothed with power from on high' (Acts 1, 7–8).

So the first point I want to make is that if institutional change is to be in accordance with the Gospel, it will require from us the ability to wait in faith and not to be in too much of a hurry to see everything clearly now, let alone to see the distant scene.

Yet there is, of course, another motif running through the New Testament: to watch, to be on the alert, so that we may recognize the Lord when he does come, especially as he invariably comes as the unexpected Messiah, that is, through events which do not conform to, let alone confirm, our established habits of thinking and feeling. Jesus chided his contemporaries for being able to read the sky for the coming weather, while they were unable to read the signs of the times. To wait upon the Lord does not mean to be blind to what is happening in front of your nose. On the contrary, it is those who do not wait upon the Lord who are blind, and when these blind claim to see, their sin remains, which is what Simone Weil was getting at in the passage from her work quoted above about finding counterfeits and being unable to discern their falsity.

And here, as a matter of filial piety, let me repeat some words of the founder of my community, Charles Gore, 'to be the inheritors of a great tradition gives men heroism, and it gives men blindness of heart'. Wonderful stuff for the radicals, isn't it? But the fact is that radicalism is no less a great tradition than its opposite, conservatism. Radicalism produces its own type of blindness. You can be enslaved to the future that never will be, as well as to the past that never was. Forgive me for emphasizing this point; I do so because by temperament I myself am a radical, a Protestant *vis-à-vis* most establishments, especially doctrinal establishments, and I try to keep myself aware of the blindness which will inevitably be mixed up with my criticisms and protests. Like a hungry dog straining at the leash, I am myself straining at the leash to tell you what I think. But I sense that I am a little too eager.

That is why on the motorway of this talk, I have begun by putting up danger signals so that you may be prepared for slippery patches on the road and not least for sudden fog.

The Kingdom of God, we would I think all agree, is not to be identified with any institutional set-up, secular or sacred. The Kingdom, or better, the kingly rule of God, uses human institutions and works through and by means of them. That of course includes the Church as a human institution, but the institutions, sacred or secular, which God uses to promote his kingly rule do not share in the absoluteness, the finality of his kingly rule itself. When any institution of state or Church is considered to possess the absoluteness and finality of God's kingly rule, what we have is idolatry. That is true of forms of government, like parliamentary democracy, concepts of law such as statute law, common law or case law, ecclesiastical arrangements like episcopacy, or the detailed articulation of what is right and what is wrong which grows up as a hallowed tradition in any particular culture or society. All these things are institutions which can be and are used to promote God's kingly rule, but they also stand under the judgement of God's kingly rule. They are partial and relative, however dear they are to us, however much we trust them for security; how-ever much in the past they can be seen to have promoted God's kingly rule, we must be ready to let them go, for their day may be over and God may now be using other means to bring in his kingdom. 'He that hateth not Father and Mother for my sake is not worthy of me' (Mt. 10.37), said Jesus, which is not to destroy the fifth commandment but to fulfil it. For loyalty to parents, to inherited institutions and inherited traditions, is no more than a school of ultimate loyalty to God, and the school does its work prop-erly by assisting us to cease being schoolchildren or their equivalent – professional old-boys. It is my private and no doubt perverse opinion that the churches contain too many professional old-boys, not to mention old-girls. That is what, in my opinion, killed the Anglican–Methodist unity scheme. Those who considered themselves to belong to the ecclesiastical Eton did not want to debase the currency by taking on the traditions of those they considered to belong to the ecclesias-tical Mill Hill. Metaphorical Etonians tend, much more than literal ones, to confuse the four-letter word Eton with the three-letter word God. And while we are thinking of Christian unity, we must consider at least the possibility that God's kingly rule may no longer in future be exercised through ecclesiastical institutions at all. For the Body of Christ is not to be confused, let alone identified without remainder, even with the sum total of all possible ecclesiastical institutions. Let me give an example: during the 1960s there were civil rights struggles in Selma, Alabama. Those who consistently fought for the right of black people to full citizenship inevitably formed a community. The community was composed of Christians of all sorts, Jews, a few Muslims and a considerable number of agnostics. The civil rights community at Selma transcended the particular religious or non-religious communities to which those present belonged. I suggest that in Selma, during this period, it was the civil rights community that was the Body of Christ through which God's kingly rule was being established. In this context, the old ecclesiastical institutions were so much deadwood. Perhaps the Church is now being called by God *to crop up*, to crop up here, here, anywhere where there is need for things to be done and witness to be borne. And it may be God's purpose that the cropping-up Church should replace the old-established institutions. This is not to deny that the cropping-up Church will in time itself become an institution. But it will be an institution very different from the institutional churches as they now exist.

I have said that the cropping-up Church will in time be institutionalized. That I regard not only as inevitable but as beneficial. Institutions are houses to live in, and we cannot do without houses to live in. But we must not be hung up on one particular type of house. We must always be prepared to move when the old house becomes unsuitable for present-day needs. One of the dangers I sense in the situation today is this. In the past, not the least important function of the churches was the institutionalization of emotional gratification. That is a terrible mouthful of jargon. What I mean is that in the past, the institutional churches provided the milieu in which people's deepest needs were met. People's undisciplined squads of emotion were given order and meaning and coherence by the structure of a church's beliefs and disciplined life. The structure supplied people's emotional needs for meaning and for reconciliation. It offered them wisdom and understanding and enabled them to feel, ransomed, healed, restored, forgiven. The churches no longer supply this emotional gratification because, by and large, they continue answering questions which nobody is asking, and offering medicines for ailments from which nobody is suffering. The result is that people don't know what to do with their emotions, hence the over-emphasis on sex, the flirtations with sadism, the lust for entertainment and consumer goods and the drugs-scene.

Since the churches no longer reveal the Word made Flesh, the Gospel has been popularly replaced by its opposite: 'And the flesh will become word; it will become the living word of God.' The phase is from Balzac's Louis Lambert. Balzac saw clearly enough that in fact the flesh can never become word; hence the growing frustration from which people suffer, and its practical consequence in the increase of crime. Clearly we must move house, but the new house we move into must be so designed that it meets people's emotional needs as they are at present felt. That seems hopelessly vague. But have we not the first beginnings of the new house in the many counselling services which have grown up all over the place – the Samaritans, the social services, welfare workers, psychiatric social workers, marriage guidance counsellors, and so forth? It is now through institutions of this sort that God's kingly rule is being exercised, and wherever they exist, they are in that place the Body of Christ.

I have mentioned the campaign for civil rights and the counselling services as examples of institutionalized change. These cropping-up churches are replacing the old-established institutional churches. This is, I know, a hard saying. But there is nothing in it alien to the Gospel. For the Gospel does not speak of endless life for existing organization. The Gospel speaks of life through and by means of death. The Gospel is the Gospel of the Resurrection, and in order to be raised from the dead, you have first to be willing to die. Unwillingness to die signifies lack of faith in God's creative power, as though, when it comes to the point, he cannot raise from the dead. There is an important sense in which, during his lifetime, Jesus of Nazareth became an institution. He became the teacher, the healer, the beloved master of a devoted band of disciples, the man who revealed God as Father and who evoked in others his own simple trust in the Father's love. As a man among men, he was the focus of God's kingly rule, the most creative and beneficial institution ever known. It was to all this he was willing to die on Calvary. For himself, as Jesus of Nazareth, he claimed no finality, no absolute validity. On the contrary, he surrendered himself. He was willing that Jesus of Nazareth should be put to death. And in the process he was willing to exchange the intimate and trustful *Abba*, who upheld him even in Gethsemane, for the cry from the cross 'My God, my God, why hast thou forsaken me?' So he passed through the grave and gate of death to the joyful Resurrection, to his ultimate Lordship. And when Mary Magdalen tried, on Easter morning, to re-establish an old and immensely valuable relationship with her Jesus of Nazareth, she was told, 'Do not cling to me.'

It is, to say the least, extremely unlikely that any institutions of Church or state will ever begin to approach the richness and value which belong to the institution they call Jesus of Nazareth. And if he gave it all up into God's hands and was willing, as Jesus of Nazareth, to disappear in death, it should not worry us too much if lesser institutions disappear and die. For death in this context is the necessary prelude to life abundant. To be willing for the old to die and to look for signs of the new being born, is to know Christ and the power of his Resurrection. For Christians, the background and context of institutional change must always be death and resurrection. That is how God's kingly rule works.

Obviously here I can only make suggestions which are no more than guesses, and no doubt what I say will be just as stupid as the notions which filled 27 heads at the meeting of the Religion and Army Committee in 1918. But I can continue in the certainty that you are all non-gullible von Hügels and my stupidity will justify itself by evoking your wisdom. Supersonic travel and instant communication through radio and television are making the world more and more into a small village. In this situation the various world cultures cannot help constantly bumping up against one another. And this means that the five great religions of the world – Christianity, Judaism, Islam, Hinduism and Buddhism – will constantly bump up against one another. In this situation I do not see how any one of these five great religions can make imperial claims for itself or continue to embark on a policy of colonial expansion. Here in England this fact has already been tacitly admitted by the Christian churches. There has been an influx of immigrants to our great cities. The churches here have not considered it their duty to try to convert these immigrants to Christianity. Many have, on the contrary, done what they could to supply these immigrants with facilities for worship according to the traditions and beliefs of their own religion. The Archbishop of Canterbury went to say his prayers in a Sikh temple in Manchester and subsequently in a Buddhist shrine in London.

What I believe is going to happen in the end (though we shall not possibly live to see it) is the emergence of a world religion, a sort of new Catholicism, based, unlike the old, not on dogma but upon the practice and experience of prayer and contemplation. When this happens it will validate the insight shown by Evelyn Underhill in her book *Mysticism*, published in 1911. She subsequently changed her view, but in this major work, she claimed that the great religions of the world were so much diverse coinage all struck from the same metal. To quote her own words:

> the gold from which the diverse coinage
> is struck is always the same precious
> metal, always the same Beatific vision of
> a Goodness, Truth and Beauty, which is

one. Hence its substance must always be distinguished from the accidents under which we perceive it: for this substance has an absolute and not a denominational importance.[3]

Behind the diverse doctrines of diverse religions, Evelyn Underhill is telling us, the actual experience of God is identical; the truth being necessarily clothed in each case with the only doctrinal garments available.

As far as I can see, the mistake made by that most readable of all learned writers Professor R.C. Zaehner is to confuse these doctrinal garments with the experience of God they seek to clothe. Zaehner does not always do this, as he is far too brilliant to be consistent. In fact the title of his great work, *Concordant Discord* concedes the point made by Evelyn Underhill. But Zaehner, every now and then, cannot resist the temptation of identifying man's experience of God with so many diverse dogmatic straitjackets. He has been criticized by, among others, Professor Ninian

[3] Evelyn Underhill, *Mysticism* (London: Methuen, 1911).

Smart. In an article in *The Times* on the Sunday before Christmas 1972, I was interested to see that Dom Aelred Graham of Ampleforth arrived at a conclusion similar to that of Evelyn Underhill in 1911.

For Christians, the emergence of a world religion necessitates a rethinking of Christology. What I find interesting is that this rethinking is already being done by Maurice Wiles, the Regius Professor of Theology at Oxford, not at all in response to the challenge of other faiths, but by what Wiles, with his profound patristic learning, considers the inherent logic of Christology itself. (He has made his first tentative suggestions here in two articles in the *Journal of Religious Studies*.) On another level, and in direct response to the challenge of other faiths, John Robinson has also some valuable things to say in his book *The Human Face of God*. And Don Cupitt has some extremely interesting suggestions in his contribution to *Cambridge Essays in Christology*. What these people are saying is this: must we not separate the Christ-reality from the historical figure of Jesus? None of them deny that Jesus revealed the Christ-reality or that he put the Christ-reality totally into practice in his human life. What they are suggesting is that the Christ-reality is not monopolized by Jesus, that we cannot identify the Christ-reality without remainder with Jesus. The Christ-reality is greater and more comprehensive than Jesus. It is focused on Jesus, but in a greater or lesser degree, it could be and is also focused on other persons as well. What then is the Christ-reality? It is the reality of God's costly, creative, self-giving love found united to his world and within it; the love which has, in varying degrees, inspired and driven men of all faiths or none. Tillich of course prepared the way here in his view that Jesus, by his willingness to die on the Cross, negated his own ultimacy as Jesus of Nazareth, in order that the Christ-reality might be revealed as the only ultimate. And this revelation is for Tillich the crucial meaning of the Resurrection.

Towards what are we changing?

I described above the cropping-up Church – the love of neighbour shown in the social concern of civil rights workers and of counsellors. But with all the immense value of their skills and loving-kindness, an essential dimension is missing here – the dimension of adoration. The point was forcibly put by Jean Daniélou at a conference in 1970 of sociologists in Rome.

> If we think that the Christian of today
> does not need to be anything besides the
> man of social or communal action, and
> that the Christian does not need to be
> the man of adoration, I say that this
> secularism would mutilate not only
> Christians, but also, all human culture,
> thus depriving man of half of what
> constitutes his greatness and nobility.

If and when a world religion emerges, its basic ingredient will be adoration. For adoration is not a hymn sandwich or a church service – oh dear me, no. Adoration is essentially contemplative prayer in which a man travels down to his own inner depths and where he discovers transcendent reality within himself, transcendent reality which is both one with his own being and, at the same time, passes infinitely beyond the limited range of his own individuality. To the degree in which one has discovered this transcendent reality within oneself, to that degree I suggest, one can under-stand what the American poet Wallace Stevens was talking about when he said, 'we believe without belief, beyond belief'. He was describing contemplative prayer as adoration. So was Bonhoeffer when he spoke of 'living before God without God'.

So I think that the churches will in due time cease to be much concerned with services and most of their other religious paraphernalia and will become schools or centres of contemplation. To date, we have progressed this far at least, that we now realize contemplative prayer is not for a spiritual elite, but that almost everybody has it within him to contemplate; but that in most cases, the potentiality has remained dormant through lack of teaching and practice. We have learnt this chiefly through Westerners gaining access to Eastern gurus. But the churches in the West are now tagging on, of which a remarkable example was the Cowley Father Herbert Slade, who in Anchorhold in Sussex taught yoga to what externally looks like a very mixed bunch of men and women.

I said above that much of the frustration of contemporary life is due to people not being able to do anything with their deepest feelings. In the sociologists' jargon, the churches are no longer providing emotional gratification. The teaching of contemplative prayer would bring release here. Not that such prayer is at all concerned with having marvellous feelings or terrible feelings. But the selving of the personality in its own depths, where it finds transcendent reality, enables people to take their feelings on board themselves, to cope with them, chiefly by the discovery that those feelings are not so important after all, since however you feel, you are aware that you are immovably founded upon the rock of reality.

So I see the churches moving in the direction of a fundamental institutional change. They will no longer be imperialist in their dogmatic claims. They will no longer provide dead services for sensitive people or hearty services for heartless people. They may no longer be one comprehensive integrated organizational structure – an aim which I believe has been grossly overemphasized during the past twenty years – overemphasized for obvious reasons. In failing to hold the people, let alone to increase their numbers, the churches have concentrated on what it is reasonable to think they can do – reassemble themselves into one organizational structure, unless indeed, the Lord God confounds their efforts as he did before at Babel. Churches as centres and schools of contemplation will not need such organizational unification. They will be servants of the people, and as servants they will not feel the need to put themselves on the books of one mammoth trade union.

When the churches have thus established themselves as centres of contemplation, then, I believe a new folk-religion will gradually emerge, which will slowly enter into and become part of the blood, not of one nation or continent, but of all people everywhere. The emergence of this world folk-religion will, of course, take centuries. (It took Christianity nine centuries to become the folk-religion of Europe.) But I think that it is in that direction that we are changing. And in the course of the change there are bound ever and again to be agonizing reappraisals in matters both of belief and morals. I don't believe, for instance, that our age is less moral than its predecessors, but simply that moral emphases have changed. Few of our ancestors kicked up a fuss about people living on starvation wages, but they did kick up a fuss about sexual intercourse outside marriage. Today that emphasis is exactly reversed.

So it will not be in peace and tranquillity that our institutions will change. Here, as always, the kingly rule of God will be a matter of challenge, conflict and victory. We shall perhaps be more aware of the sword of Christ than of his peace. But that is only another way of speaking about death and resurrection.

THREE

A Rose by Any
Other Name

The theme of this chapter may seem arrogant. And perhaps it is. But that is a risk worth taking. It is a plea to those who believe themselves called actively to participate in the Decade of Evangelism to have their eyes open to the presence of God.

Bringing people to God does not consist of persuading them to accept a package-deal of information about him. In any case, people do not need to be *brought* to God. He is the Infinite Mystery in whom they already live and move and have their being. (We talk of the Mystery as 'he' only as a matter of convenience, just as we talk of human love as 'it' without meaning that love is a commodity like coal.)

If God is the 'he' in whom people already have their being, it follows that true evangelism consists of helping them to become aware of the environment in which they are already living. The revelation of the Mystery is thus a deeply personal matter. It is not an ecclesiastical affair, but the enhancement of a person's sensibility so that he or she may begin to recognize a dimension which can be obscured by what is more obviously apparent, like perceiving in the campanile at Pisa only

that it leans. A world-view, or at least the beginning of one, may or may not gradually be con-
structed from such an enhanced sensibility. But
most crucially the sensibility will be focused on
one particular and maybe small area of a person's
life: an experience, say, of a heightened peace and
happiness, or some deeply felt anguish which calls
out for an ampler vision of our human predicament, or an inner demand to know why we feel
urged to do something for others at considerable
cost to ourselves. Such particular occasions often
lead to a more widely extended sensibility which
will make a person want to discover the ultimate
ground, the final criteria of truth or right, in loyalty to which he may find it necessary to reject the
conventional God of the ecclesiastics.

Ivan Karamazov comes to mind here. What, we
may ask, was the moral imperative which com-
pelled him to return his ticket to eternal bliss?[1]
Was it not God within Ivan which drove him to
condemn a God in whom he had been taught to
believe? Such a God might exist, but he was not

[1]   Fydor Dostoevsky, *The Brothers Karamazov*, trans.
Constance Garnett (London: Heinemann, 1968),
p. 252.

good enough. And a God not good enough was no God. He was a human artefact whose power over men Ivan did not deny. What we have here is God's revelation of himself to Ivan in terms of a moral intuition which could not be denied.

What hinders us from perceiving Revelation as a deeply personal matter is the claim of the churches to have it cut and dried in dogma. 'Dogma', said Martin Buber, 'even when its claim of origin remains uncontested, has become the most exalted form of invulnerability against revelation.'[2]

Christian dogma does indeed accept that 'un dieu défini, c'est un dieu fini'. But its coverage is so wide that we are left with very little room for our questing agnosticism. The situation is reminiscent of words in St John's Gospel: 'If you were blind, you would have no guilt; but now you say "We see", your guilt remains' (Jn 9.41). The claim to extensive knowledge about the Divine and its operation in the world is here castigated as a source of evil. For to advertise a human artefact as if it were the living and ultimate Reality is to

2   Martin Buber, *Between Man and Man* (London: Kegan Paul, 1947), p. 18.

make people blind to what and where they most truly are. They may conclude that they have no need of God because he has been represented to them as a specific object, and as such has for them no meaning and hence no attraction or power. Grandiose representations of the Divine block out the vision of Ultimate Mystery, for the Mystery in fact is to be found not in a metaphorical Out There, but in what at the deepest level we ourselves most truly are. That is because the human spirit is what it is only because it is indwelt by the Divine Spirit, so that the Divine reveals itself by means of our own self-discovery. That is why God's revelation of himself must be deeply personal.

How can God be both himself and me? It is true that in earthly things and in the thought-forms devised to describe them there is an absolute difference between identity and otherness. But in our relation to heavenly things such demarcation does not apply. Here complete otherness admits of the deepest identification (as indeed what we call the Athanasian Creed tries somewhat lumberingly to express). God can thus be both the me and the not-me, and it is only by discovering him as the me that he reveals himself as the not-me. It was St Catherine of Genoa who said, 'My me is God, nor do I find my selfhood save in him.' Recognition of God as the me prevents us from making him into an artefact. For what I most essentially am can never become an object for inspection.

We must proceed by way of concrete examples. For what is profoundly personal can be described only by what happens to persons. The occasions depicted may often seem inconsiderable, if not trifling. But we must not allow the noise of the church organ to make the still small voice seem trivial.

Passing a row of houses, each with its small front-garden, it is not uncommon to come across one garden which is superbly kept. It witnesses to an urge to create order and beauty on however diminutive a scale. As such it is a manifestation of the human spirit, and the human is here at one with the Divine, for the Divine is the source of all order and beauty. The householder tending his garden is thus engaged in an act of contemplation and worship. That is why he finds his work so satisfying. His motives may to a small extent be mixed. Perhaps he will derive pleasure in having a better garden than his neighbours. But what worshipper in church or pious person on his knees can claim to be totally pure in heart? In his instinctive feeling that his work in the garden is worth doing for its own sake, and in the delight with which he surveys the result of his labours, the householder is responding to the value of God revealed. The revelation is not invalidated by the absence of accompanying informative clutter. Indeed, the Word of God can be drowned by chatter about its nature. The appreciation of value is one form of God's revelation of himself to us, and it is enough that the value of order and beauty has been intuitively apprehended.

The impulse to make something through our efforts the best thing we can is a response to the value of self-giving in terms of hard work to achieve a desirable end. And it is a revelation through the human spirit of the Divine. 'My father worketh still, and I work' (Jn 5.17). That statement operates today. The Father works in the person who works. Wherever the dignity of labour is intuited (if not intellectually understood) by the labourers, there God is revealed and there he is being served and worshipped. That is true not only of the householder working in his own garden or the craftsman working in his own shop, but of the workforce in a large industry.

The greatest challenge to industrial management and to union leaders on the shop-floor is to give the workers a sense of the value of what they do, to make them feel that they are not just hands but essential contributors to the manufacture of something worthwhile, just as, at least in past centuries, the common foot-soldier felt he was contributing something of value to his country's honour. The ultimate task of management and trade union officials is to reveal the holy, not in any pious sense but in terms of instilling in the workforce a sense of the value of what they are doing, not only as a service to the community at large but in itself as productive labour. For this sense of value is God within them. The all but superhuman difficulty of inspiring this vision of value is not being underrated. (It may often seem like one of those things of which it is said that with man it is impossible, but not with God.) What is being stressed is that in an industrial plant, no less than in other places, it is possible to hold infinity in the palm of your hand and eternity in an hour, however little it may be conceptualized in those terms.

The realm of value is of course as wide as life itself. But at this stage our concern is with those values which are common to everybody, and not those dependent for their appreciation on, say, an ear for music or an eye for painting: endowments which not everybody possesses, however important they are for those who do.

The industrial plant may stand for work and the front-garden for rest. (For rest in its most important sense consists of unimpeded activity, doing without let or hindrance what you most enjoy, which means that many people already at times have experience of that Sabbath rest which remaineth for the people of God.)

But there is another universal experience of mankind, and that is people's relation with one another.

Our relation with most people is inevitably superficial. They are for us little more than objects around us. If they minister to our convenience we can treat them with common courtesy. If they stand in our way we can, with varying degrees of subtlety, push them aside. If they prop up our self-esteem we can extol their wisdom and say how much we trust their judgement. If we feel denigrated by them we can turn what they are and do into evidence against them. As far as we are concerned none of them exists as a person in his or her own right. They are so much furniture for our use or clobber to be disposed of.

But we cannot maintain all our relationships on this superficial level. Without any of our willing or planning we may find ourselves becoming more deeply involved with somebody who crosses our path.

A story is now going to be told. It requires no apology. Jesus spoke in stories, and it ill becomes us to pride ourselves on being more sophisticated than he was.

For a long time Mary passed an old woman who lived near her, giving her no more than an automatic smile. Then, by chance, Mary was present when the old woman fell down and twisted her ankle. With others, Mary went at once to her aid. She needed not only to be helped up but to be assisted home. Mary found that she lived alone and needed somebody to take her to hospital. This Mary felt urged to do and stayed with her until she could be brought home again. She discovered her name was Miss Wilson. It was obvious to Mary that her task was not yet finished. Miss Wilson needed looking after. So Mary used to call on her every day to set her house in order and do her shopping. From one point of view this became an irksome chore. Mary was already busy enough with a complicated timetable, and Miss Wilson was just another complication. How unlucky she was to be passing when Miss Wilson fell! But this somewhat taxing and certainly irritating situation had another side to it. Miss Wilson was a very ordinary old woman, but Mary began to grow fond of her. She began to be aware of Miss Wilson's value as a person, demanding though she often was. And in perceiving Miss Wilson's value Mary felt herself enriched as though something of value in herself, hitherto dormant, had been woken to life. On Miss Wilson's side, she was obviously grateful for what Mary did, not only for its practical benefits but because in Mary's caring for her she was able to appreciate something of her own worth by appreciating something of Mary's.

What in fact each of them had discovered in the other was the holy. Most certainly neither of them would have described it in those terms. But when you have the reality, does nomenclature matter very much? 'A rose by any other name ...' In terms of value, God in each of them had gone out to God in the other. They had each of them become places of worship. When they met, the Beyond was in their midst.

In a sense, however, the relationship between the two of them remained on the periphery of their lives, even if it did reveal a measure of the holy. But with some people we are totally involved – spouses, children, lovers. The outwardness of these people has been internalized by us so that what we are and do tastes of them as the wine must taste of its own grapes. For better or worse, they are part of our own identity.

The ambiguities which result when people are this closely related are a matter of common knowledge and experience. Because we love them deeply, we can also hate them, since we are all subject to the usual psychopathologies of everyday life, with their resultant confusions of feeling. To say with Sartre 'L'enfer, c'est les autres' is too simple a diagnosis. The torturing rub is that in this context of closeness the other is generally heaven as well as hell. Having tasted heaven we cannot let it go, in spite of all the hell it brings. What we call a satisfactory relationship, say an averagely good marriage, is one in which heaven predominates, maybe to a degree in which to all intents and purposes hell is vanquished. For the harrowing of hell is not a strange meta-physical event in some other world. It occurs whenever in a human relationship love overcomes whatever opposes it.

This harrowing of hell is one of the most encour-aging things about human life. It is the victory of life over death, an everyday Easter – common-place not because it lacks glory but because of its frequent occurrence. It can happen that even in the most neurotically entangled relationship some element of uncorrupted love somehow passes along the wires. Even here, perhaps espe-cially here, we can witness the more-than-human splendour of resurrection. For to love deeply, even if that depth of love is not returned, is to participate in the Infinite Mystery in which we have our being.

It is true that such love can in part be attributed to biological urges. But is not sexual chemistry itself mysterious? We have not disposed of it simply by saying that it exists to propagate the species. Sexual attraction must be much more than utilitarian, if only because it can lead to the appreciation of value – the value of the beloved as an unfathomable and sacred mystery. The importance of a path does not lie in its existence as a path, but to the place to which it leads. Sexual attraction may be necessary, but it is not an end in itself. Its end is the revelation of value. And where value is revealed, there God is revealed, not as some isolated, if not bizarre, experience but as the common coin of human existence.

When people try to make love for God into an escape from the vicissitudes of human love the result is invariably a chilling inhumanity. Turning God into what is in fact a *faute de mieux* inevitably turns our alleged love for him into a similar substitute. The Ultimate Mystery, if we are truly to apprehend our participation in it, must be Mystery Incarnate, so that in us and others God is made man. We can find him only in ourselves as we go out to him in others. We cannot find him in some imagined empyrean. That is why

> He prayeth best, who loveth best
> All things both great and small.

For the habitation of the Mystery we call God is not confined to people. It can be found in countless forms.

It often happens that we feel wedded to the house or town in which we have lived for a long or significant time. We may have been happy there or have suffered, probably both. In themselves these places can be far from beautiful or noble, but they have become part of what we are. And because our own identity is mixed with them, they can for us be holy ground. Our feelings for them may be as ambivalent as our feelings for people. We can hate them because we also love them. Like a marriage, they have been experienced both as a home and a prison. Maybe our reaction to them is entirely negative, in which case all we can do is to leave them behind and try to forget them. But more often we find ourselves entertaining a kind of affection for the places where we once belonged. The good things which have befallen us there are more alive to us than the bad. So the place is perceived as testifying that life is worthwhile because it brings us what we have learnt to value. It is felt as a sacrament of selfhood, not of the superficial ego, grasping because threatened, but of the deepest self which is at one with the Divine. And because the place is for us such a sacrament, it reveals the ultimate Mystery to which we belong. In our affection for it, vague though it may be, there is enshrined a love for what is more than earthly. It may elicit from us no grand thoughts or words. 'It was fun', we may say, 'going back to Peckham. It made me feel a bit weepy, but it was ever so nice.' The words will indicate an intuition far more profound than this verbal attempt to express it. For it is not easy to marshal feelings into thoughts which can be uttered. Perhaps one of the less noticed and more important *trahisons des clercs* is that contemptuous dismissal of the apparently banal without attempting to perceive what lies hidden there. They may preach eloquently on the text 'Surely thou art God that hidest thyself', but, they assume, there are limits to the forms in which God is hidden. How can it be something described as ever so nice?

Where there is not contemptuous dismissal, there can be suspicion bordering on contempt – fear, in fact, rationalized as discrimination. Here we are concerned not with bricks and mortar, but the light of setting suns, the round ocean and the blue sky. Wordsworth's apprehension of the natural world as the revelation of God is apt to bring a superior smile to the faces of religious aficionados. But it is incontrovertible that many people perceive the face of the Divine in the splendours of nature. From time immemorial it has been instinctive for man to lift up his eyes unto the hills from whence cometh his help. 'The world', said Simone Weil, 'is God's language to us.' We hear that language when the holy in us goes out to meet the holy enshrined in the scene before us. We find ourselves caught up in a dimension which transcends the fears and schemes of our superficial selves. Our heart is filled with wonder and love. We know we belong to what we see, that in its very otherness from us it is also part of our very selves. Here to look at what is before us is to worship. For we are aware of Mystery which cannot be gainsaid because we are enfolded in the love which it inspires. From one point of view what we see is an object – the scene with which our eyes are confronted. But as it grips us it loses its character as an object because we begin to perceive it as underlying and confirming our own truest identity. Home is where we belong; and contemplating the splendour of what we see, we recognize our home. Does it matter if we fail to call it the gate of heaven or do not think of connecting it with the God in the straitjacket of theological definition?

We can concede that if Wordsworth had lived in the tropics, the natural world would have revealed to him divine mysteries other than those he perceived in the English Lake District, perhaps the vision of irresistible and unaccountable power vouchsafed to Job; and indeed this might have prevented him writing the tamely conventional verses of his later years. But we must accept the testimony we have, not conjectures about what we might have had.

A testimony parallel to Wordsworth's was made by Vaughan Williams after he had attended a performance of *Die Walküre* in Munich:

This was my first introduction to later Wagner, but I experienced no surprise, but rather the strange certainty that I

had heard it all before. There was a
feeling of recognition, as of meeting an
old friend, which comes to us all in the
face of great artistic experiences. I had
the same experience when I first heard an
English folksong, when I first saw
Michelangelo's *Day and Night*, when I
suddenly came upon Stonehenge or had
my first sight of New York City – the
intuition that I had been there already.[3]

Vaughan Williams may have described himself as
a cheerful agnostic, but clearly when it was sacra-
mentally bodied forth for him in sound or sight
he was intuitively sensitive to the Mystery in
which, like us all, he lived. He recognized his
home.

It stands therefore that it is the Mystery we call
God which we experience in the places to which
in one way or another we feel we belong, be
it the streets of Peckham, the hills and lakes of
Cumbria, or in the presence of great art. Beneath

[3]   Ursula Vaughan Williams, *R.V.W. A Biography
of Ralph Vaughan Williams* (Oxford: Oxford
University Press, 1964), p. 30.

the surface of our generally often feebly descrip-
tive words there lies the instinctive if uncon-
ceptualized insight: Surely God is in this place.

*　*　*

It is sometimes said that aesthetic experience is
for many people a substitute for religious experience. The statement is a matter of semantics. If by
religious experience we mean the use of some
ecclesiastical apparatus, a prescribed set of ideas
and practices, then the statement is true. But if by
religious experience we mean the apprehension of
ultimate value, then the statement is manifestly
false. No ecclesiastical edict can exclude God
from picture gallery, concert-hall or theatre, and
it is undeniable that it is ultimate value which
people can find there.

It is not (as we said) given to everybody to have
an eye for painting or an ear for music and drama;
but for those who possess the necessary sensitivity aesthetic experience reveals a dimension not of
this world. What they see or hear can fill them
with blessedness and love. They can be caught up
in what is worship because something of final significance has been shown forth and apprehended

61

not as alien to them but as expressing what they most truly are. That is the secret of their delight which declares, albeit obliquely, 'That glorious not-me is also me.' Once again we have God in them responding to God present in the other, that is, in what they see or hear. It is true that the savage negativities of life are not absent from aesthetic forms. The music may be violently turbulent, as in Vaughan Williams' Sixth Symphony or the chamber symphony written by Shostakovich after his visit to devastated Dresden. The painting may represent horror as in Goya's *Witches' Sabbath* or *Saturn Devouring one of his Children*. The drama may be *Lear* or *The Wild Duck*. But the grandeur of the aesthetic form puts a question-mark over the evil it portrays. It hints at the possibility of transfiguration. It speaks a nevertheless: the nevertheless of value found in that by which value is destroyed. We may go away purged by pity and fear, but our chastening leaves us more truly because more cleanly ourselves. That is how the composer, painter or dramatist of genius points the way to redemption. He destroys our illusions, but in facing hard reality we find worth, so that death itself is made to reveal life. The artist has so used his medium that we experience what destroys as that by which our life is enhanced – in Christian symbolism, the life-giving Cross.

Here we must take notice of the report that some of the guards at the Nazi concentration camps spent their evenings listening to Beethoven's quartets. What this reveals is the division of the human personality into watertight compartments. It was not unique to the Nazi guards. We can, for instance, find an example of the same thing in a seventeenth-century Capuchin friar, Father Joseph, who was a master and teacher of contemplative prayer, having himself attained its highest form, the unitive way. Joseph was the collaborator and executive aide of Richelieu in his campaign to make the Bourbons predominant in Europe by means of the savagery of realpolitik – treachery, torture, war and massacres.[4]

This watertight compartmentalization of the self is a horrifying aberration, but on a miniscule scale it will not be unfamiliar to those who have lived among lovers of the arts or people of prayer.

4   See Aldous Huxley, *Grey Eminence. A Study of Religion and Politics* (London: Chatto & Windus, 1941), *passim*.

It has been said that comedy is God's fifth columnist sabotaging the earnest in the cause of the serious. Mercifully, just as there is a psychopathology of everyday life, so there is a comedy of everyday life. The essence of comedy in its contemporary meaning of humour is a sense of the incongruous, like Mrs Malaprop's combination of intellectual pretension and ignorance. By showing how comic is the solemnity with which we adhere to our illusions of grandeur – intellectual, moral, spiritual, social, as the case may be – humour delivers us from our thraldom to them and throws us back to reality. It is by humour that the proud are scattered in the imagination of their hearts, with false pretences shown up, so that an authentic sense of value may take their place. In man's ability to perceive and laugh at the comic in himself and his world, the Divine is at work creating order. For there can be no true order without a sense of proportion, and what destroys our sense of proportion is pride. Laughter is the enemy of pride as pride is the handmaid of illusion. 'Pride', said G.K. Chesterton, 'is the downward drag of all things into an easy solemnity. It was by the force of gravity that Satan fell.' In this context, to laugh is to be redeemed. For the laughter is felt as a return home from the far countries to which we have exiled ourselves. To be hurled into that journey may at first be an unpleasant shock. But the shock is one of recognition – of what we really are. To laugh at the incongruity between our assumed persona and our genuine selfhood is the beginning of a recognition that our selfhood requires no protection from our persona because the self is rooted in the Ultimate Mystery which is both ourselves and Other.

But incongruity can reveal what we are in an even more important way. As Peter Berger has reminded us,[5] what makes us laugh are often the very things which cabin and confine us. What is it that makes our narrow limitations, the harsh realities which constrict us, the prisons of this or the other kind which are part of our human lot, seem funny? Is it not an intuition that we belong elsewhere as well, and that the contrast between the here and the there, to both of which we belong, is inherently comic? Peter Berger has described humour as providing signals of transcendence. We laugh because of our intuitive realization that

5   Peter Berger, *A Rumor of Angels* (New York: Doubleday, 1969).

the rocklike necessities to which we are bound are inconsistent with some glory which is also ours. That is why death itself, the black humour of a corpse and the whole paraphernalia of the under-taker's trade, can lighten the heart with laughter. Laughing at our constrictions, including the final constriction of death, is not far from worship-ping. It is an unconscious lifting-up of our hearts to a reality beyond us which we unknowingly rec-ognize as ours.

It was said above that when in the name of justice Ivan Karamazov handed back his ticket to eternal bliss, it was God within him which led him to this renunciation. Whenever the distinction between right and wrong is recognized the Divine is pres-ent. That does not mean that such moral evalua-tions are necessarily correct. They may be danger-ously uninformed and false. It is in the awareness that an absolute distinction exists between right and wrong, and that right has an immediate and total claim upon us, that the Ultimate Mystery can be discerned. This is a much-ploughed field which hardly needs exploring here. Did not Wordsworth describe duty as the 'stern daughter of the voice of God'? Where anybody recognizes his duty and does it, there the Ultimate Mystery is revealed, even if he fails to say 'Lord, Lord', and may be mistaken in his estimate of what his duty is. It is reported of John Huss that when an old woman in righteous wrath cast a log onto the fire around the stake to which he was tied, he said '*Sancta simplicitas*'. He recognized the presence of God in somebody who in her ignorance considered it a righteous act to contribute to his torture. Moralists can be reckless and unmerciful people. We could do worse than heed the gentle warning given us by Muriel Spark in a newspaper interview. Asked by Allan Massie, 'Would you call yourself a moralist?', she replied, 'Yes. I do have this feeling that everything matters a great deal, but ultimately nothing matters so very much that we should forget that we are human.'[6]

* * *

This chapter – a plea that we should keep our eyes open to the presence of God in areas which are neither ecclesiastical nor technically religious – could be summarized by a statement of Simon

6   *The Times*, 1 August 1987.

Rattle, the conductor of the Birmingham Symphony Orchestra, about music. For what he says applies equally to the Divine.

> The most dangerous thing to do to something that relies on peripheral vision is to stare it in the face. There are some things one has to glory in their tenuousness, and music is one of them. That's why so many of us are not enormously verbal. If you try to pin it to the wall, you've had it.[7]

To this we could add the words of the prophet Isaiah as found in the Authorized Version: 'I am sought of them that asked not for me; I am found of them that sought me not' (Isa. 65.1). But the correct translation (as found in the Revised Standard Version) may be equally true of a missioner: 'I was ready to be sought by those who did not ask for me; I was ready to be found by those who did not seek me.'

[7]   *The Sunday Times*, 21 January 1990.

FOUR

What I Believe

It all began with the sheep and goats. It was a dream. I was reading in St Matthew's Gospel the parable about the Day of Judgement on which the sheep are put on God's right hand and the goats on his left. I was astonished and dismayed to read as follows:

And he shall set the sheep on his right
hand, but the goats on the left. Then
shall the king say unto them on his right
hand, 'Come ye blessed of my Father,
inherit the kingdom prepared for you
from the foundation of the world: For
you believed virtuously in my virgin
birth: you believed loyally in my physical
resurrection – flesh, bones, heart, liver,
kidneys, all wonderfully spiritualized; you
went faithfully to church every Sunday;
you said your prayers regularly every
morning and evening: you gave up
reading the novels of Mary Wesley
because they were too sexy: you stopped
buying a bottle of plonk for the family's
Sunday lunch, and gave the money saved
to help train a priest.'

I then noticed that beside me there was a dustbin full of rotting food. I wondered why it was there until I saw that the Bible I thought I was holding was in fact a hunk of putrid meat. As I was about to throw it into the dustbin, I woke up.

I turned on the light. I was still enough under the spell of the dream to get out of bed and take down the Bible from my bookshelf. I wanted to be reassured. My agitation made my fingers clammy so that it took me several minutes to find the closing section of Matthew 25. What should it say? To my relief I read:

> For I was an hungred, and ye gave me
> meat: I was thirsty and ye gave me drink:
> I was a stranger, and ye took me in:
> Naked and ye clothed me: I was sick,
> and ye visited me: I was in prison, and
> ye came unto me.

And reading on, I noticed (as I had often done before) that the sheep, the people who had done these generous things, had no idea at all that they were engaging in a spiritual activity, serving and worshipping God.

I got back into bed and switched off the light. But I didn't sleep. The sight of the dustbin of rotting food and the hunk of putrid meat haunted me. But I also sensed that something of considerable importance had been revealed to me. And I had to work out not so much what it meant (that in a sense was only too obvious), but how to fit it not only into the context of my own life but much more into the wider context of how a lot of people worship and serve a God of whom they are unaware. Why, I asked myself, were they unaware of him when in fact they were serving him in a way which was the truest worship? Was it because they found the god advertised by the religious aficionados lifelessly unreal when not positively nauseating?

I had been set a problem I could not evade. I wasn't fool enough to imagine that I could solve it to anything approaching completeness. It was dauntingly complex, involving matters not only of theological doctrine, but of how people felt and thought both as individuals and as members of society. And this in turn involved the rise and fall of political and economic ideologies, not to mention the scientific and technological environment in which we all live. The problem, in short,

73

consisted of a gigantic set of Chinese boxes. Perhaps I could glance at one or two of them, if even as much as that.

Of one thing I was certain. We were not living in an era more godless than those of the past, not, that is, in real terms. There were just as many who belonged to God's right hand as there ever were, even in the days when the churches were crowded and new ones had to be built instead of existing ones closed down.

I didn't want to write as a monk. Monks and nuns often have severe problems of their own, but they aren't my concern here. In what I say I shall try as far as possible to imagine myself as an ordinary member of the churchgoing or non-churchgoing public. And if occasionally I mention something which has occurred in my own religious community it will be because the same thing can be found among the faithful who go to their parish church. In any case, monks and nuns are not a spiritual breed apart, lifted up above the common run. They are quite ordinary mortals, and they are self-deluded if they consider themselves more spiritual than those outside their compound. So perhaps, I thought, it wouldn't require a great deal

of imagination to picture myself without a cowl
and scapular riding as one passenger among many
on the Clapham omnibus. That at least is what I
felt compellingly that I ought to do.

It would, I think, be useful to start by giving a
very brief sketch of the two main contexts in
which as an adult I have lived. In the most general terms there was a considerable contrast
between the two. As a young curate in London
and as a member of the Community of the
Resurrection at Mirfield I have lived among
churchy people for whom God is to be found
predominantly in church, with all the doctrinal
apparatus this involves in terms of printed
prayers, forms of service, hymns, and so on.
Without church these people feel cut away from
God. Here at Mirfield, for instance, there is every
day a Mass at 10 a.m. for the elderly and infirm.
One day through some muddle there was nobody
to say the Mass. By chance I happened to pass by
that way. I found the old men in a state of deso-
lation, looking like the people described by St
Paul as having no hope and without God in the
world. I mention this incident not because I want

in any way to look down on the old people I saw. They are far better monks than myself and have done more in their lives for what they believe to be the Kingdom of God than I have ever done. I mention it simply to illustrate how for them, in their feelings if not in their theological reflection, no church meant no God.

The same attitude can be found in parishes. As servants of God's Kingdom what the faithful want above all things to do is to bring other people to church. Parish missions are organized with this express intention. The presumption is that people who don't go to church are without the God they need to fulfil their lives. How, then, are they to find him? By being persuaded to come to church. It is of course natural for the clergy to take this view. Of whatever concern any healthy-minded person is in charge, he quite rightly wants it to be as flourishing and successful as it can be. So the greater the number who come to church the better, quite naturally, the parson is pleased, and the more convinced he is that in his parish at least God is starting to win.

What I am trying to do is simply to describe this identification of God with church services, not to denigrate it. Church services, I know, have been an inspiration and source of renewal and strength to thousands of people. When I was a curate in London at All Saints, Margaret Street, hard-worked people, or people living under considerable strain of one sort or another, or happy young people who were students or shop-assistants, or old people who were feeling the disabilities of age, all sorts and conditions of men and women, used to write and tell us what a joy and re-creation it was to attend our High Mass or Evensong, and how they went away feeling equipped as they weren't before to cope with life. So I am aware from my personal experience of how God can and does give himself to people when they worship him by means of what goes on in church. And this remains gloriously true in spite of the few to be found in most parish churches (and religious communities) for whom religion in the sense of church is what Freud (wrongly, of course, in my view) said religion always is – an obsessional neurosis. Such people think, speak, plan and fantasize about nothing but church, as golf or railway fanatics drive you mad with boredom as they endlessly expatiate on their particular cult. But the abuse of something is no argument against its proper use, even if the corruption of the best is the worst.

When I am in London I stay in Chelsea and attend church at St Luke's, Sydney Street. And I would like here to testify how much it means to me to worship there. If I find God anywhere it is in that church at the Holy Communion. I sense his presence as soon as I enter the building, and on leaving I am aware that I have known, in however small a degree, what it is to rejoice with joy unspeakable and full of glory.

I mention this to underline that fact that I have no urge or wish to speak slightingly or in any way to pillory those many people for whom God is felt to be present and most real by means of what goes on in church. But these are not the only people who serve and worship God, standing with the sheep at his right hand. And this brings me to the second context in which I have lived.

As a don in Cambridge I found myself among colleagues most of whom were not at all religious in any technical sense. It is true that a number of them were devout Anglicans, Roman Catholics, Free Churchmen and Jews. But these were in the minority. There were also a few who would describe themselves as Christian or Jewish believers, but didn't attend any place of worship – that is, on any regular basis. The great majority, however, were what an earlier age would have described as free thinkers – people for whom the God of the churches meant little or nothing. Some of them were avowed atheists, but most of them were agnostics. They could not accept the claim of organized religion to possess such certain and detailed information about Ultimate Reality. ('Poor little talkative Christianity', as E.M. Forster said.) But their agnosticism worked both ways. Unlike the atheists, they were as chary of dogmatic denials as of dogmatic assertions. As trained researchers in science or the humanities, they were aware that truth could be betrayed by over-hasty conclusions. They understood that valid discoveries could be made and authentic facts established only by the willingness to accept the unease of suspense. Most of them were aware that life contained a dimension which transcended the world of sense, but they considered themselves unequipped to describe what it was, and they were unwilling to accept the oracular descriptions provided by this or the other religious institution. Their attitude was summed up in a charmingly characteristic remark I once heard made by G.M. Trevelyan when he described the typical religion of Englishmen as that 'which eschews dogma and is content to live broadly in the spirit'.

Both the atheists and the agnostics had thought out what they believed. But there were also those untroubled by speculation of this kind. They were content to get on with the business of living without considering the ultimate issue it raised. They had no metaphysical itch. But it would be wrong to say that they didn't care. About certain things they cared deeply – the quality of their research, for instance, and the authenticity of its results; or the need of somebody in distress of this or the other kind. Indeed, in terms of Jesus' rule 'By their fruits ye shall know them', they were as much on God's right hand as the technically religious. They may not have said 'Lord, Lord', but, without realizing it, they were certainly doing the will of their Father which is in heaven.

Looking back, I can see that this was tacitly taken for granted by those dons whose religious devotion was deep and genuine. It often happened that their oldest and closest friends were agnostics or atheists. Yet no attempt was made to convert them. Evangelism stopped short at friends of this kind. Their disbelief was respected and honoured.

In fundamentals the technically religious felt themselves to be very much on the same side as the technically non-religious. For what mattered supremely to them both was the personal integrity which showed itself not only in their insistence on the highest standards of scholarship but also in the general conduct of their lives, not least in their practical concern for colleagues who were ill or the victim of some other form of adversity.

Perhaps in passing a commonly held error should here be laid to rest. It has to do with what is familiarly described as academic malice. Dons in fact are not more malicious than other people. An equal degree of malice can be found among those who faithfully attend their parish churches or are members of religious communities. The difference is that dons, being clever, can often express their malice in phrases which are memorable for their wit, while the others clothe their malice in turgid phrases about the will of God or the welfare of Christian brotherhood. A much more important difference is that the dons recognize that they are being malicious and may take a considerable pride in the witty phrase by which their malice is expressed, while the others are often taken in by the religious paint with which their malice has been coated. But this is only to say what the technically religious are the first to insist upon, at least in formal and general terms, that we are – all of us – sinners.

I have described the main contexts in which I have lived because they help to explain the significance of my dream about the sheep and goats. My concern here is not to bore the reader with any of the subtle psychoanalytic implications of the dream. It is true that dreams are allusive and refer to a hundred different things. But they can also have one overriding meaning which is blatantly obvious. So it was with the sheep and goats. The sheep were orthodox pious churchmen while the goats were non-churchgoing people who were likely to be agnostics or atheists. But this assessment was revealed as putrid. It simply would not do and had to be thrown away. The dream in fact only summed up what from the Cambridge context of my life I had long since recognized but which in some degree had been overlaid by the churchy atmosphere in which I am now living – that many of the technically non-religious belonged beyond a peradventure to God's right hand.

What, then, had this to say about an age often described as godless? One thing it emphatically did not say. It did not say that unbelievers were in reality believers in disguise. Those who were convinced atheists did not in some hidden and obscure sense believe after all in the God worshipped by Christians and Jews. And those who were agnostic, open to the possibility that there might be some sort of something which could perhaps be called God, were not Christian believers without knowing it. That trick has been tried and seen through and need detain us no longer.

But if from the technically religious point of view unbelievers are exactly what they say they are, that does not in any way rule out the possibility that, in terms of the parable I dreamt about, the unbelievers may be with the sheep at God's right hand, and in that sense godly.

For there is nothing ultimate about belief and unbelief in credal statements. Such statements are no more than attempts, and all too easily misleading attempts, to point to realities which can no more be intellectually captured and encapsulated than sunlight can be carried in a string bag. And these realities can be apprehended in a variety of ways on a variety of levels. Belief in the sense of intellectual assent to credal statements is only one way on one level, and a somewhat superficial level at that. For which of two people is the true believer – the person who gives intellectual assent to the statement that God is love but does nothing for a friend in need, or the person who does not believe there is a God but who puts himself out to help this same friend? St John's Gospel speaks of *doing* the truth, and the sheep at God's right hand in the parable are all people who have done the truth without knowing it – 'When saw we thee an hungred and fed thee?' It is these who are shown to be godly in the true sense, unbelievers though they are.

The words of Simon Rattle about music [quoted in the previous chapter] might well be applied to belief in God:

> The most dangerous thing to do to
> something that relies on peripheral vision
> is to stare it straight in the face. There
> are some things one has to glory in their
> tenuousness, and music is one of them.
> That's why so many of us are not

enormously verbal. If you try to pin it to
the wall, you've had it.[1]

To make music as Rattle does with the
Birmingham Symphony Orchestra is the equivalent of doing the truth. It requires confidence in
the value of making music, but that is something
taken for granted. And it requires the costly discipline of submission to the laws and principles by
which music is adequately interpreted and per-
formed. But the result is its own justification. No
need is felt for any speculative of metaphysical
underpinning. It could be said that so it is also
with the truth which is done – the hungry fed,
the sick visited, and so on. The deed is seen to
justify itself without the pinning to the wall of any
theoretical statement about it.

When I said earlier that I didn't believe we were
living in an age more godless than any of those of
the past I meant there were as many people today
who were doing the truth as there ever were. It is
by their works that they show us their faith, even
if in conceptual terms they have no technically
religious faith at all. Without too much abuse of

1   *The Sunday Times*, 1 August 1987.

language they could be described as people who are religious without religion. This is a hard saying for churchmen because it seems to put a big question-mark over their activities. Yet this is not really so. There will always be large numbers – more, we are told, than those who attend football matches – who (like myself) find God and worship him in a St Luke's, Sydney Street. My concern here is with the people who don't. It is a plea for a greater understanding of this considerable majority who have no technical religion, make no use of religious agencies and who claim either that they do not believe in God or cannot believe in the God presented to them by the churches, or who frankly admit that they do not know what they believe and in any case do not consider arrival at credal conclusions of much importance.

Churchmen are apt to respond to such attitudes by claiming that what people believe affects what they do, pointing by way of example to the horrors of the Gulag or the Nazi concentration camps and gas chambers. But the persecution and massacre of Jews and dissidents were not invented by Hitler and Stalin. They merely took over and continued what the Christian Church had done for centuries. The horror was greater because technology had made the processes of cruelty and murder more efficient. But the will to persecute and slaughter was in the first instance the will of Christian believers. And if we now find such activities totally abhorrent so that it is painful for us even to think of them, that is chiefly due to the rise of secularism and the consequent abandonment of Christian orthodoxy. This needs to be remembered when we consider Muslim militancy. What in these days differentiates Muslim from Christian militancy is that from the point of view of Western culture the Muslims are two or three centuries out of date because no secularist tradition has taken root among them.

Of course it goes without saying that what a person believes affects what he does. But what Christians now believe about tolerance and the sacred right of individuals to discover and continue to hold their own convictions about ultimate truth owes much more to people like Voltaire and John Stuart Mill than to any Christian thinkers – an example, if ever there was one, that the sheep at God's right hand need not be orthodox believers or churchmen.

What then should be the attitude of churchmen to those who are outside the Church and who are indisputably the unbelievers they say they are? And what should churchmen try to do for them?

I have already pleaded for a greater understanding of them, and I wish now to repeat with as much emphasis as I can that the first and most important thing we can do for them is to try not to convert but to understand them. Attempts to convert often border on a lack of respect for an individual's personal identity, while that identity is reverenced by attempts to understand. How can we expect people to understand what we are saying if we do not ourselves try to understand what they are saying? True evangelism consists of receiving as well as giving, and it is better that it should do nothing but receive than nothing but give, for then giving is a euphemism for mental and emotional bullying.

Can we therefore discover why people whose goodwill and generosity are at least equal to that of Christian believers are not religious in the technical sense, and may either not believe in God at all or whose belief is so tenuous that in conceptual terms it amounts to very little?

Any attempt to answer that question must be limited by the experience of whoever attempts it. So nothing comprehensive can be expected from one individual. But that does not mean that whatever testimony he is able to give is without value, however random or selective it must inevitably be. With luck it may at least stimulate thought and encourage others to bear their complementary witness.

For some people belief in what is called a personal God is an insurmountable obstacle.

With generous honesty an Anglican priest from a solidly clerical background has written:

> I thank my God that I have never been
> burdened with any sense of being in
> touch with Jesus or God as with a
> person. Percolated, inspired, possessed,
> created – yes; but the analogy of human
> relationships has never been reflected in
> my experience of God. Perhaps
> clergymen's children have a particular

difficulty with this imagery – in which
case I am not complaining![2]

The important words here are 'analogy' and
'imagery'. To say that God is personal could be
called a *façon de parler*. It is not a direct or photographic description of him. It merely indicates
that in the Ultimate Mystery we call God there is
something which in some way or other corre-
sponds to our experience of human personhood.
It is on a par with the statement of the poet that
'My love is like a red, red rose.' The poet is not
here suggesting that his mistress *is* a rose *tout
court*, but simply that her loveliness can meaning-
fully be compared to a rose's loveliness. She could
be described in many other ways by means of
many other images. So it is also with the Ultimate
Mystery we call God. The Christian mystics have
often described him as the fount or source from
which we continually flow. He is the ocean of
which I am a wave, the sun of which I am a shaft
of light, the tree of which I am a branch. In these
images the Divine and the human, God and man,

[2] Andrew Henderson, in Eric James (ed.), *Stewards of
the Mysteries of God* (London: Darton, Longman &
Todd, 1979), p. 64.

are not two different objects. The human is indeed derived from God, but in such a way that God is present and active in what man is, so that man would not be man unless God were thus present and active in him, just as the wave would not exist without the ocean, the shaft of light without the sun, or the branch without the tree. What I experience is a reality great enough to be God and intimate enough to be me.

Yet the churches in their forms of service, hymns and sermonizings continue to speak of God as personal as if it were the same unambiguous sense in which the boss of a business corporation or a paterfamilias is personal. He insists on being obeyed, his instructions being whatever a particular church at a particular epoch says they are. He likes being flattered and cajoled. In a bitterly humorous letter to a friend, George Tyrrell said that a Christian is expected to behave towards God like a mouse which, when confronted by a cat, squeaks out:

> O lovely Pussy!
> O Pussy my love,
> What a beautiful Pussy you are,
> You are,
> What a beautiful Pussy you are.

It was of course exasperation which led W.R.
Inge, who had no ear for music but as Dean of St
Paul's had to listen to a great deal of it, to protest
that he could not believe in a God who liked
being serenaded. Yet there is more to the remark
than vexation. For worship is invariably understood by Christians to refer to church services
(and so to singing), and its object appears to be
the paying of compliments to an exalted celestical
magnate who has us totally in his power and who
needs to be urged to have mercy on his impotent
subjects. I am not suggesting that this is how the
majority of a congregation understand what they
are doing. Probably far from it. But an outsider,
listening to what is said and sung, would have
every reason for concluding that it was.

Many years ago I was given what for me was an
unforgettable example of how easy it is to forget
that we can call God personal only by way of
analogy or imagery, and to assume that personal
is a direct photographic description. I was dis-
cussing forms of government with a priest who at
the time was the extremely competent and efficient chaplain of a Bishop of London. Kingship,
he said, was obviously the most Christian form
of government, as God is king of the universe.

I was reminded of Lichtenberg's aphorism that God made man in his own image and man has returned the compliment.

Of course in these days God is most frequently represented by the churches as a very loving person who suffers with and for the sake of his children. Books of devotion often have titles like *That Tremendous Lover* or *Enfolded in Love*. Indeed, this emphasis upon God as the ultimately loving person has largely extinguished belief in hell. No loving person, it is argued, would want to see somebody he loves suffer eternal torments. So God will go on loving until human defences are broken down and a responsive love elicited. And if the cost of this operation is suffering untold and unimaginable, well, God has borne it and (since he is eternal and always the same) continues to bear it. This is most beautifully expressed in the old poem now sung as a hymn:

My song is love unknown
My Saviour's love to me
Love to the loveless shown
That they might lovely be.

It would be difficult to discount the moving power of lines like these of which the visual equivalent is the picture of Christ upon the cross.

> We may not know, we cannot tell
> What pains he had to bear
> But we believe it was for us
> He hung and suffered there.

My purpose is not in any way to criticize or belittle sentiments of this kind. To do this would be ridiculous were it not utterly shameful, for nothing is more true of our human experience than the affirmation that greater love hath no man than this: that a man lay down his life for his friends.

My intention in describing the representation of God as the ultimately loving person is to emphasize that it does not meet the difficulties of those for whom belief in a personal God is an insurmountable obstacle. We may wish that such people were other than they are and hope that they will change. But meanwhile we must respect them enough to try to understand the difficulties they now experience. What are they saying? For most of them those difficulties are not intellectual but existential. They spring not from any strongly held metaphysic but from their experience of life.

Except on the most superficial level the relationship of one person to other persons is never straightforward. It always involves ambivalence. In the secret places of the heart, hidden very often even from ourselves, we hate the people we love and are attracted to the people we hate. This is often due to reasons which could be described as objective: other people are not morally perfect, nor have they reached a state of total emotional maturity. Hence we intuit that in their attitude and behaviour towards us they are not only being genuinely beneficent and generous but are also in part playing their own game at our expense. And by this we are not only offended but damaged. We sense that in part we are their playthings, used to put on a performance whose purpose is their own gratification. So we love them for their genuine beneficence and generosity and hate them for using us as pawns for their own satisfaction. Conversely, we may be the object of somebody's undisguised malice or anger. And for this we hate him, but our hatred is not unmixed. For our enemy here is able to display and articulate the

degree of his malice or anger without the reserve
and inhibition by which we are dogged and cannot shake off. So we envy his ability to throw
restraint to the winds in a way we cannot do. We
find it attractive. And although we may say 'I'm
glad I'm not like so and so', what we mean, at
least in part, is the opposite. There is a great
deal of psychological insight in Oscar Wilde's
remark that 'wickedness is a myth invented by
good people to account for the curious attractive-
ness of others'.

So far I have described what could be called the
objective reasons for the ambivalence which char-
acterizes our relationships with other persons.
Those others always in actual fact have mixed
motives, their concern being only partly for us
because it is also partly for themselves. But the
relation of person to person is even more complicated than that. For the road which leads from
one person to another is haunted by ghosts which
refuse to be exorcized. We see a person not only
in terms of what he actually is in the present but
also in terms of what other people have been in
the past. We are in this sense the victims of our
own objectivity. It is as though our past experience of others, especially in very early days, has

fixed upon us distorting spectacles which we cannot take off, so that when today we encounter AB our spectacles make him look uncommonly like the XY we encountered on a distant yesterday, and we react accordingly. It is one of the most devilish things about human life that we are thus the prisoners of our personal history. We are confronted continually by new people and new situations, and we respond to them again and again as though they were those same old people and same old situations by which years ago we were damaged. This phenomenon of projection is encountered most glaringly in those who run through a series of marriages, but in some degree or other it is universal. Wordsworth's description of objects in the external world as 'what we half create and half perceive' is true in a sense he did not envisage of the people with whom we have to engage on any but superficial levels.

The most serious level is that of love. If it is not true literally, then it is certainly true in many other ways that each man kills the thing he loves. If, for instance, our dominant experience of love is love of the possessive kind, then love is a murderer and we want to murder it in return. It refuses to let us stand independently on our own two feet and is always attempting to hold us up so that our integrity compels us to kick it away. Or our experience may be of a love which seeks its own in terms of compliance to its own wishes and desires, exercising upon us an emotional blackmail which makes us feel guilty when we refuse to pay up. Of this the most pernicious form is what is claimed as suffering love: 'Look how much you make me suffer when you fail to respond to me as I want you to.' It makes us feel brutes, as it is intended to do, when we choose the freedom by which alone we can grow into our full stature. Then there is experience of conditional love of the more direct kind. It has to be earned. We shall be loved only to the degree in which we conform to a prescribed pattern of behaviour or achievement. So much deviation from this pattern means so much less love. And there is always the love which fails, and this we can experience both as its givers and recipients. We can love people for what they are not, that is, for the image we have projected upon them which is far from the reality of what they are. And they can love us for the same reason. When the image is seen not to fit, love dies.

It is the baffling complexity of personal relationships which makes it impossible for many who have been injured by it to believe in a God who is personal. For such belief is felt to entangle them yet again in a malaise they are courageously seeking to outgrow. It is the cowards who, as the price required to continue believing in what they assume to be traditional orthodoxy, are prepared to remain submerged in the muddy waters of pathological distortion. The others have decided that if belief in a personal God requires them to remain clamped to injuries and sickness they are beginning to leave behind, then integrity requires them to have no truck with him.

It can obviously be argued that such people, however great their courage, are intellectually mistaken. The personal God is not subject to human frailty. He has no mixed motives. His love is totally generous and is in no way adulterated by the self-regard which pollutes human love. His relation to us is straightforward. It is completely free from those hidden agendas found in human love. When we approach him as personal we have to think away those imperfections and pathologies too often found when humans relate to each other. To the degree in which we intellectually understand his total freedom from all ambivalence, to that degree we shall be able to be freed from our own.

Would that it were so. But the facts are otherwise.
For there are large areas of our being where the
writ of our intellectual discernment does not run.
And in these areas the discrimination of which
our intellect is capable, thinking this or the other
away, is not possible. When Pascal said that the
heart has its reasons which the reason does not
know, it is generally understood (as indeed Pascal
meant it to be) as a truth beneficial to faith. But
it works equally the other way round. With our
reason we may accept that God is this and not
that, but the reasons of the heart may tell us
otherwise. And the reasons of the heart are more
fundamental and powerful than those of the
brain. We are in large part the creatures of our
experience, and it is in the heart (to use Pascal's
term) that our experience makes its most forceful
and lasting impression. What we may consider the
triumph of intellectual truth over intellectual
error can leave the heart virtually untouched.

So it can all too frequently happen that whatever
somebody is told about the God who loves him
and suffers for him, it can mean to the person so
informed only something horribly similar to the
human love whose claim to love and suffer is a
form of blackmail. And he can accept no more

of that. He may be able to accept an Ultimate Mystery in which we live and move and have our being, but not a God who is out to evoke responsive love. And in a paradoxical way such a person is, from the Christian point of view, intellectually correct. For God's love is certainly not of the possessive and blackmailing kind. In his inability to believe in a personal God who loves him, he is therefore, in a twisted fashion, bearing witness to Christian truth.

Although far less fundamental, he may also have reasons, not of the heart, which the reason does indeed know. For from what he sees, his intellect may bring him to the conclusion that a great deal of talk about God's love looks suspiciously as if it were compensatory. Starved of human affection or the sexual love for which we are made, a person may try to make up for it by fantasies of God as a human lover. It is indeed true that human affection and sexual love are the vehicles by which God's love is transmitted to us. They are what Christians call sacramental. But to identify divine love with human things which transmit it is to make an idol which cannot deliver what is required of it, and the result is obvious frustration. Stendhal is more realistic

101

when he makes his hero, Julien Sorel, say of the declining affection of his mistress: 'What is the use of a love like this? One might as well take to religion.'[3]

The complexities surrounding belief in God as personal illustrate how necessary it is for Christians to be ready to receive from unbelievers as well as to give. They must be ready to take the criticisms of unbelievers seriously (which will often require seeing through the rationalizing clothes in which they are dressed) and entertain the possibility that their own apparently Christian belief has at least in part succumbed to the distortions which for the others make unbelief necessary. For the unbeliever may be like somebody who has concluded that he has no use for classical music because he has only heard it played incompetently so that it is no more than a noxious noise. Such a person would be intellectually correct. Beethoven's music is not what he has heard.

[3]   Stendhal, *Scarlet and Black* (*Le Rouge et le noir*) (London: Penguin, 2000).

Closely related to the area of personal relationships is that of guilt. Although the churches
are less the guilt-merchants than they once were,
they are still moderately efficient purveyors of it.
And it is still a not inconsiderable stumbling-
block to belief in the churches' God, especially
among those who were brought up in a religious
household but have subsequently given up religion as an intolerable oppression.

As a child of 10 or 12 I was myself perplexed by
what seemed to me a most unfair illogicality. I
was taught that the bad things we did were
entirely our fault, while the good things were the
result of God at work within us, and we could
therefore claim no credit for them. The moral
dice thus seemed very much loaded against us. As
moral agents we were capable of evil but not of
good. This belief is still implied when we are
exhorted to follow the Christian practice of self-
examination. What we examine ourselves to discover are the sins we have committed so we
may ask for God's forgiveness of them. It is
seldom suggested that we should discover the
good things we have done. It is as if we were
required to be like hypochondriacs looking eagerly
for every sign of illness while we disregard all

103

manifestations of health. Church services auto-
matically include a confession of sin, placed
generally at the beginning, as if we were always
and inevitably dirty and in need of a shower
before we can engage in social intercourse with
God. Christians sometimes feel most guilty, not
because of any sins they are aware of having
committed, but because they cannot remember
any.

It is hardly necessary to say that there are those
who do not care whether they have done wrong
or not, and consider any sort of moral investiga-
tion a stupid waste of time. They are what they
are and that is the end of it. Like the adolescent
gang in *West Side Story* they may even take a certain pride in being no damn good. But the unbelievers we are considering are not of that ilk. They
are deeply aware of themselves as moral agents
capable of choosing between good and evil and
fully admit that there are occasions when they
freely choose the evil rather than the good and
are thus culpable. What in fact sticks in their gul-
let is what they see as a lack of moral seriousness
on the part of the churches, because the churches'
estimate of sinfulness is too slapdash and taken
for granted. They notice (as we have seen) that it

is taken for granted as a matter of theological theory that sins have been committed and need forgiveness since the last visit to church, even if that were only yesterday or the same day. Hence the statutory confession. And the sins themselves seem often regarded as a kind of laundry-list, so that we feel dirty when in fact we are clean and clean when in fact we are dirty. A man may feel guilty, for instance, because he has badly lost his temper with his wife, for loss of temper is on the laundry-list. Yet maybe this severe loss of temper is the most positive and constructive thing which has occurred for years in his marital relationship. It has broken through an atmosphere of artificiality by which true love between him and his wife was slowly being suffocated. It was the triumph of reality over pretence. Yet it is felt and confessed as sin. Conversely a man may give up a mistress (as did St Augustine of Hippo) because fornication or adultery is on the laundry-list, feeling that in this area at least he has ceased to sin, while in fact he is guilty of the most abominable callousness towards the woman he has abandoned, leaving her to suffer without mitigation the anguish of love withdrawn as he throws at her a one-way ticket from himself to nowhere.

It is this sort of formality in assessing sin and guilt which leads those outside the Church to condemn it for its lack of moral seriousness. Rules of thumb may be convenient, but they do little except deceive, not least in the illusion they give of enabling people to know where they are.

It is only when moral responsibility is treated as involving the immensely complicated issues it in fact does that a valid assessment of real guilt for real evil can be made.

Perhaps the greatest complication is the distinction between guilt which is realistic and that which is pathological. The existence of one does not cancel out the existence of the other, however closely in particular cases the two are generally intertwined. It is obvious that if a man confined to a wheelchair feels guilty for not jumping into the sea to save a drowning child, then his guilt is pathological. But the wheelchair may be taken as an image for infirmities which are not necessarily physical, and the drowning child as an image of all those in peril of being submerged in a sea of troubles. I can, said Kant, implies I ought. The difficult question is whether or not I can. What I feel I ought to do may be within my moral and spiritual capacities, and, if so, my guilt at my failure to act is realistic. But maybe what I feel I ought to do is beyond my capacities, in which case my guilt at my failure is pathological. That is a fundamental distinction, however difficult it is to establish. And it is not cancelled by our alleged tendency to give ourselves the benefit of the doubt. How often in any case do we do so? In public we may defend ourselves, but our feeling the need for self-defence may indicate that within us the verdict has gone the other way.

It might be useful here to mention the exploitation of pathological guilt to a degree not usually found in the mainstream churches, but to which they adopt an attitude of benevolent neutrality and often of active support. I refer to those professionally organized religious campaigns which set themselves up from time to time. One of their most characteristic features is the refusal to distinguish between pathological and realistic guilt. It is understandable, since the whipping-up of pathological guilt is one of the campaign's most effective weapons. Make a man feel that his whole self is morally and spiritually at death's door, and he will eagerly take whatever medicine is offered him. That his personal integrity, not to mention his intrinsic tenderness, has thus been violated passes unnoticed. He has been bludgeoned into religion, and that is the result desired. The end justifies the means.

It is to the great credit of church leaders that they do not themselves indulge in this sort of exploitation, and indeed are especially careful not to, for which they are often condemned by the more zealous and less discriminating of their flock. But church leaders stop short of postively censuring exploitation of this kind. If it brings people to church, what have they to complain about?

There is, too, a factor of wider importance. I referred earlier to those who do not care whether they have done wrong or not, insisting that they are what they are and that is the end of it. This rejection of moral responsibility finds a bogus justification (as though desire for justification were not a contradiction) in the vulgarization of the discoveries about the human psyche made by Freud and his successors. Freud, for instance, insisted on the necessity of self-control and in general had a deep sense of moral responsibility. But he is misinterpreted as holding that a person is no more than his neuroses, so that all feelings of guilt are pathological with no place left for guilt of the realistic kind. This parody of his teaching has become part of the common consciousness of unthinking people, and it leads to the conclusion that we are not to blame for whatever we do or fail to do. We cannot help being simply our own damned selves. In such a situation it is essential to stress that human beings are not simply the victims of their compulsions, but still retain a large measure of free will, making them capable of choosing between good and evil. The danger here is the familiar one of the swinging pendulum. Since the area of pathological guilt has been grossly exaggerated, it may lead to a similar exaggeration of realistic guilt, especially as this has the added attraction of seeming straightforward in a no-nonsense manner.

When church leaders appear to condone the exploitation of pathological guilt, it reinforces the conviction of many thoughtful non-churchgoers that the churches lack moral seriousness. Anything goes, so long as it results in increasing the size of congregations.

So far, our concern has been with people in the context of their personal and private lives. But there is also what could be described as inclusive guilt, that is, the guilt either of a whole society or of some group within it. And here there is far less concern to distinguish what is from what is not our fault.

When, to take an example, Marilyn Monroe committed suicide, a cleric in a published statement said that the responsibility for her death lay with all those men whose lust had led them to enjoy her films. As I am by orientation homosexual, I did not myself feel the prick of guilt (though I wondered whether I could be held responsible for the fast driving of James Dean which led to his death in a motor accident at the age of 24!). But in some men such a statement was bound to stir up pathological guilt about their natural instincts and affections, said to be implanted by God. And it would certainly encourage the view that the churches' estimate of guilt was slapdash.

That, however, was a one-off occasion, important only because it revealed underlying proclivities. For the churches are indeed unhappily seen as somewhat reckless and haphazard in what they say about sexual morality.

So much continues to be written about sexual mores that one hesitates to add to it. But the issues raised cannot be totally evaded. It is true that from one point of view sex is a most private and personal matter; but in terms at least of marriage and divorce it must also rank as one of the primary concerns of society as a whole.

Non-churchgoers, or those who have abandoned going, are frequently those who have been indelibly dyed by attitudes to sex which they have inherited but which may no longer be current in the churches. But the attitudes stick, and defiance of them does not remove them. A telling if somewhat crude example can be found in a pamphlet for lads written by a member of the Mirfield Community some 60 years ago: 'Don't entertain an unclean thought. It may destroy you.' Nobody would write that today. But the residue of such an attitude lingers on and can cause a great deal of pathological guilt. It is only aggravated by the guilt-feelings which are aroused in any case when a boy or girl begins to claim sexual equality with his or her parents. Unfortunately, such adolescent fantasies are seldom completely left behind, but continue, unacknowledged, to hover like a miasma around a person's life. The irrational guilt-feelings they engender can be activated when some cleric begins to bang a gong about sexual wickedness. 'I cannot in good conscience go to church when clergymen say that sort of thing', is not an entirely unreasonable attitude when what is claimed to be loyalty to Christ's standards is seen through as the crass insensitivity it in fact is. Irrational guilt about sex in terms of overperformance, inability to perform well or at all, unwillingness to perform, is one of the important causes of marriage breakdown which the churches are seen to foster in so far as they foster pathological guilt about sex.

Another stumbling-block, at least with regard to the Anglican and Free churches, is that edicts on matters of sexual morality change. People thus discover that for years, in obedience to the Church's teaching, they have been loaded with heavy burdens and grievous to be borne which are subsequently declared unnecessary. The use of contraceptives by married couples is an important example. An elderly widow once said to me: 'Our married life was less happy than it could have been and less fulfilled because we obeyed what the Church taught about contraception. Now they have changed all that. It seems we were born too soon.' Another example is the attitude to divorce. In the past a divorced person who remarried, or a single person who married a divorcee, was forbidden to receive Holy Communion. Now priests themselves are allowed to remarry after divorce.

I personally give an unqualified welcome to these liberalizing changes. But when the Church, claiming by definition to speak with authority, says one thing yesterday and something contradictory today, it can hardly complain if its authority is regarded with less than total respect.

With regard to homosexuality the position is even less stable, for with homosexuality it is not only a matter of then and now but also of here and there. The physical expression of a deeply personal and permanent relationship between two people of the same sex is sanctioned by some bishops and condemned by others. Here it is not a case of he that has ears to hear let him hear, but let him take care what he hears and where.

It is not my purpose to argue for any particular views about sexual morality (though my statement that I welcome liberalizing tendencies indicates that I have them). My concern is to point

113

out that the Church's teaching on these matters is not consistent. In general it seems sometimes to encourage the stirring-up of pathological guilt about sex and sometimes to be aware of that danger so that it takes steps to avoid it. And in particular, it seems to say different things at different times and in different places about contraception, divorce and homosexuality. If this were seen as caution in the face of immensely sensitive and complicated issues and an unwillingness to arrive at hasty conclusions, it might well elicit the sort of respect born of sympathy, which is the deepest sort. But what the advocates of different views appear to have characteristically in common is the dogmatic certainty with which they enunciate them. The situation could be described by a rhyme of W.S. Gilbert's with only the first line adapted:

And anxious clerics you might meet
In twos and threes in every street
Maintaining with no little heat
Their various opinions.

How seriously can they be taken?

* * *

The same question arises when church leaders pronounce on political and economic issues. I am not denying that it is the duty of the churches to work for a socially and economically just society. The Kingdom of God is a social reality or it is nothing, and churchmen have an obligation to point out the injustices which militate against it. Was it not Gladstone who described the social conditions of the kingdom of Naples as the negation of God? It is, as Newman said, the Church's business to interfere with the world, even if it fell to his rival, Manning, to do so effectively. The point is too obvious to need labouring further.

But there is a trap here, often pointed out and as often disregarded. To point out what is wrong with a society is not the same thing as to espouse one political remedy among others as the only one which is morally right. This is what most church leaders seem to have done in Britain. It would have been better had they taken to heart the warning given many years ago by T.S. Eliot in his Boutwood Lectures. The Church, he said, must always point out what is wrong in a society, for what is wrong is always unambiguously wrong. But it must be chary of pointing out what is right because that is a matter of contingency, that is, of what is possible

115

and not possible in a given situation. Politicians may often be faced with the necessity of choosing what is right in the form of a lesser evil which prevents a greater one. Their judgement may well be at fault, but that is no reason for considering their policies wicked. There was a profound moral seriousness in Rab Butler's statement that politics is the art of the possible. The shrill advocacy of what is claimed as political righteousness can often be irresponsible when it is divorced from the nitty-gritty of actual political predicaments.

A further example of a similar irresponsibility is the application of a double standard. Tyranny and denials of freedom pass unnoticed when they occur in black African states, while in South Africa they bring down howls of execration. They are morally wrong wherever they occur, but many English churchmen seem to think that what is sin in South Africa is virtue in Mozambique.

The real relation of pathological guilt to the stirring-up of what is called a political conscience needs to be examined. It could be said that fundamentally pathological guilt is guilt about being alive at all, and this is always mixed with realistic guilt about failures of conduct which can really be

avoided. But both can be submerged in the com-
munal zeal of a public crusade against the wickedness of other people. A person's irrational guilt at
being alive at all makes him feel fundamentally
without value. This state of affairs needs to be
recognized not only on the intellectual level but
in the secret places of the heart, and thus recognized it can be worked through and dissipated.
The excitement of a political crusade does no
more than gloss it over, leaving it securely in
place. Thus if a crusade succeeds in what it sets
out to do, a new crusade has to be found. Unless
it is, the pathological guilt once again reasserts
itself in all its wretchedness. The point was neatly
summed up in a cartoon in the *Spectator* which
showed two pictures of the same person. In one
picture he is wearing a T-shirt with the slogan
'Free Nelson Mandela', while in the other he
wears a T-shirt marked 'Free ——'. The person's
concern is thus shown to be not the injustice of
which Mandela was a victim but the need to join
in a crusade in order to forget wounds which
need to be healed not ignored.

When complaints are made that churchmen
should concern themselves with their spiritual
functions and leave controversial public issues

117

alone, it may often be because politicians find demands for social righteousness inconvenient. But that is not the whole truth. One of the Church's primary missions is to heal the sick in mind and soul. To heal sickness is not the same thing as to use and exploit it, even if the exploitation is negative in the sense of supplying a method, in this case a political campaign, by which sickness can be temporarily forgotten, thus offering a palliative rather than a cure.

In this area the positive exploitation of guilt works less well than the negative. It consists of telling us that almost everything wrong with the world is our fault. We are rebuked for the existence of nuclear weapons, even if they were first used before we were born. We are upbraided for the contrast between the poverty of the third world and the wealth of the first, as though it were a matter of our individual choice and management. If there is starvation in Eritrea we are made to feel it is almost entirely our fault, even though there are already too many supplies for the relief agencies to distribute. If in London there are many homeless people, the cause, it is indirectly inferred, is the secure comfort in which we ourselves live. Even the weather is now our fault, since it is due to the pollution of the earth's atmosphere to which we have contributed.

Nobody disputes that such things need to be put right and that there is a moral obligation upon us to do all we can to see that they are. But the dynamic behind effective action is the challenge to make things better. The nature of this challenge can be discerned by the challenge, say, of making a garden out of a wilderness or of climbing Everest. The existence of the wilderness is not felt to be our fault; nor is the height of Everest. The compelling urge to make the garden or climb the mountain is due to the sense that these things are worth doing for their own sake and has no connection with pathological guilt. If it had, the enterprises would not get very far. For the nature of such guilt is to bring on a torpor of wretchedness after its initial punishing effect has worn off, so that we only toy at action and soon give up even that.

Mercifully the activation of this guilt by means of the sorry state of the world seldom works efficiently even though the sorry state is rationally acknowledged. But the stupidity of trying to arouse guilt in this way is not a good advertisement for the Church, nor does it increase confidence in its spokesmen.

It may look as if I am out to condemn church-men. But I understand that it would be absurdly unfair to them not to recognize that, like every-body else, they are caught up in moral complexi-ties it is not easy to unravel, and it is an infirmity common to us all to yield to the temptation of cutting the Gordian knot. My concern is to try to understand why people of goodwill and gen-erosity often find signing up with the Church either pointless or inconsistent with their personal integrity. I am here suggesting that one (there will be others) of the reasons may be that they find a lack of fundamental moral seriousness in much church talk and that this conclusion is not entirely illusory. If I have painted the picture in broad strokes, it is in order to make its outlines clearer.

When the churches speak of God as personal there can be a further difficulty which sometimes includes guilt, but without its being central.
Images of God as a person are often accompanied by images of hierarchy, that is, of a society organ-

ized in classes ranked one above another. For centuries it was a telling image. Society was hierarchical, with the king at the top of the pyramid. In time it came to be felt that there was a qualitative difference between a king's family and lesser people. Royalty only married royalty. Inevitably this provided a picture which, with its various ramifications, was applied to God. God was king, the Trinity (its strict theological definition was too cerebral for it to appeal to the heart) was a sort of royal family with the Virgin Mary co-opted into it as Queen Mother. The saints were princes and nobles who attended upon the king in heaven, while the angels were superior servants who, as is the way with superior servants, made ordinary mortals feel small and under-done.

It was still a telling picture almost up to the First World War. For society continued up until then to be organized hierarchically. Those considered the highest in the land were considered also the best in the original meaning of aristocracy as morally and personally the most excellent, for daylight had not yet broken into magic and the press ignored the peccadilloes of the upper classes. A king was still considered as belonging to a different species from his subjects, so that Queen Mary, for instance, when her husband ascended the throne, considered it one of her most important and most difficult tasks to make her children realize that he was not only their father but their king.

Hymns of the Catholic variety continue to represent heaven as life at court, where princes and nobles can be asked to catch the king's ear, while appeals are made to the compassionate heart of the Queen Mother to intercede on our behalf with her son who to her will grant favours he would not grant to us.

Protestants, on the other hand, would have none of this. The Reformation abolished the celestial court, thus impoverishing the religious imagination. But the Reformers made up for it by concentrating on the notion of absolute monarchy. The absolute monarch must in our estimation and practice be allowed to be absolute. Let God be God, said the Reformers, sternly warning us against any encroachment on the crown rights of this Redeemer. Heaven thus became less cosy. It consisted only of God in his everlasting seat remaining God alone. The imaginative context in which this picture was painted can be seen in the Preface to the Authorized Version of the Bible which is addressed to 'the most high and mighty Prince James', who is subsequently invoked as 'most dread sovereign'.

To be sure, none of this imagery, Catholic or Protestant, is theology in the strict sense of the term. But theology so considered has only the limited appeal of mathematics. What informs and touches the deepest places of heart and mind are the pictures by which God is represented. Pictures of a hierarchy once spoke powerfully to people. But today they no longer do. They have lost their potency because we no longer think or feel about society in hierarchical terms. King's courts belong to history where we can be amused by their corruption and enjoy the toadies they spawned, while absolute monarchy conjures up pictures of Hitler and Stalin.

It is not only in the higher reaches of government that the sense of hierarchy has faded. Fathers are no longer the stern and remote figures they once were when Sir Thomas Bertram returned unexpectedly to Mansfield Park and reduced his grown-up children to panic. Their word is no longer law. What father today would consider it his duty, as did Mandell Creighton, Bishop of London (he died in 1901), to be the one person of whom his sons were afraid? Children these days regard their parents as being very far from those set above them to command. Brides no longer promise to obey their husbands, as the man is no longer considered the head of the woman as St Paul took for granted from the social structures of his time. Domestic servants (where they exist) no longer consider themselves inferior to those who employ them; on the contrary, the cleaning lady regards herself as the benefactress of those for whom she works, showing a touch of *noblesse oblige*. Headmasters no longer inspire dread – in one of the most ancient and prestigious public schools the senior boys now call the headmaster by his Christian name. And in general the belief that Jack is as good as his master is no longer a sentiment of defiance, but is considered an ordinary fact of life which requires no comment. Few bosses now have the unfettered power to hire and fire, and they are considered as functionaries, not as God Almighty.

The whole notion of hierarchy belongs today only to the world of fairy-tales. Once taken for granted like the air we breathe, it has disappeared from common consciousness, and when on rare

124

occasions it is found, it is considered an historical curiosity.

But the churches refuse to relinquish these lifeless images because their sacred books, liturgies, and hymns are saturated with them, and they have not the creative imagination to put others in their place – admittedly a tall enough order in all conscience. The result is a sense of unreality in much ecclesiastical worship, as when an outsider finds himself among a group of strangers who have their own slang and jokes as they play their own private game.

It is true that attempts are sometimes made to invent verbal forms which bring God down from his royal loftiness, presenting him as the sort of nice friendly bloke we might meet in a pub, the rich man's guest, the poor man's mate. But these are excruciatingly banal, capable only of making one squirm and of being promising material for comedians who still think the Church worth sending up.

Because images of hierarchy are dead, those who make the experiment of going to church find themselves confronted not so much with what they consider untrue as what seems Ruritania or Disneyland.

For some, however, this may not be so. An image may continue to speak, but no longer with beneficent power. It can be malign. This can be particularly the case of the image of God as an absolute monarch which sometimes still lurks somewhere in the recesses of the mind. It can conjure up visions of absolute tyranny. The implication is that I must do what the monarch says, simply because he says so. Preachers often pronounce that something is God's will without explaining why it is, or how righteousness as an absolute value of its own is what we mean by God present within us as most truly ourselves.

Many thoughtful people see exhortations to obey Somebody Else for what they are – the destruction of morality. For to do something simply in obedience to what somebody else says is not a moral act, even when the somebody else is God himself. Morality is not a matter of obedience to an external command. For an act to be moral it has to be in accord with a deep inner conviction that it is right. That is what Kant meant when he said that a man is himself the legislator of the law he is

126

morally bound to keep. He acts morally when he acts in accordance with his own moral convictions, though he can choose not to. When Antigone, against the orders of King Creon, buried the dead body of her brother, she appealed to a law eternal in the heavens.[4] But the appeal sprang from a sense of right deep and ineradicable in her own heart – great enough to be God, intimate enough to be herself – and that was what made her act moral.

For such an apprehension of true morality there is no need for a person to have studied Kant or to have read Sophocles. It is often instinctual; and it leads to the conclusion (if you are lucky) that talk about obedience to God's will is less than convincing. If, however, this moral instinct has been submerged by exhortations to obey Another, you find yourself in the grip of a tyrant, feeling guilty if you do not obey him and miserable if you do.

An example of this confusion of a moral act with an act of obedience to another can be found when churchmen put themselves under what they

4   Sophecles, *Antigone.*

call a spiritual director. That in itself is a wise and responsible move, for our fallibility invariably needs the counsel of somebody more experienced and judicious than ourselves, who is not encumbered by our own blind prejudices. But the decision we arrive at in the end must be our own for which we ourselves must take full moral responsibility. Integrity forbids us to hide behind the spiritual director we have consulted, loading on him the responsibility which is ours alone as we say: 'My spiritual director knows what I am doing and he approves.'

Here we have the ghost of the hierarchical idea manipulated for our own ends.

But in its heyday the sense of hierarchy depends chiefly on the realities of power. When the king could cut off your head if you disobeyed him, it was difficult not to believe that might is right. Plain historical fact made it impossible for the Church to present Jesus of Nazareth as the wielder of such coercive force, so he was projected into the future as an omnipotent dictator who at the end of the world would come again with irresistible might and destroy those who had disobeyed him – a belief overpoweringly displayed on the wall of the Sistine Chapel. Righteousness as obedience to what was claimed as God's will thus became a form of insurance, with brewers in the nineteenth century still building churches as fire-escapes.

Today, the threat of power as coercive force can no longer be used to draft people into the proffered safety of what passes for goodness. We have seen too much of power as force to be impressed by it. We have seen it used as the instrument of unqualified evil. So the God of such power can no longer be the God for us, whether in the form of wonders and portents, or, as here, as the ultimate guarantee of what is right.

Yet it is power as force which gives to hierarchy its ultimate sanction. If the lowly do not obey the lofty, they must be made to, or punished. That is a postulate we can no longer accept, and it leaves an important set of ecclesiastical images lifeless.

In an attempt to understand why it is that people of goodwill and generosity cannot accept the God of the churches, suggestions have been made in which pathological guilt has played a significant part, either at the centre of the stage or hovering in the wings.

Attitudes must now be considered in which such guilt plays no part. These attitudes are predominantly intellectual, to do with the head rather than the heart. That is not to deny that they can arise from an existential predicament, but to emphasize that they operate in the daylight of the conscious mind. Their working-out belongs to the domain of reason, even if it is the heart which sometimes sets the problems.

No doubt there are many issues of this kind, but three in particular call for attention because of their universality. They are the attitudes of mind created by the natural sciences, the growing familiarity in our global village with other great religions, and the fact of suffering. A great deal has been written about all three. But they are too important to ignore, even if it is not necessary to consider them at any great length.

Science as popularly conceived is not only science. It is also myth. As such it is vaguely felt to be the

answer to all problems. Men in white coats holding test-tubes are the symbol of a panacea waiting
to be discovered. When it is, the millennium will
be ushered in. Scientists in their laboratories are
its forerunners. Faith in the myth still lingers,
even though it has been radically shaken by the
invention of nuclear weapons. Old assumptions,
however, die hard. It is still often assumed that, in
time, science in the form of psychology will
invent ways of extinguishing the destructive
instincts of mankind. What in the old days God
was unable to do, perhaps science now will. And
if such a hope goes against the evidence, what is
faith for?

Few thoughtful people today hold this millennial
myth, but as its legacy it has left a degree of faith
in science as a saviour, or at least as the best saviour we have. It is a realistic faith which does not
ignore what militates against it. It produces a
confidence which is not too sanguine and a hope
not too optimistic. It is admitted that the discoveries of science may destroy the world, not necessarily cataclysmically by the use of nuclear
weapons, but gradually by choking the earth and
its atmosphere with the indestructible rubbish
produced by the technology which science made

possible. But there is one advantage: such a disaster is foreseen by scientists and they can suggest remedies for it. They have thus become the prophets of the modern world, warning us of the consequences of what we do, whether we will hear or whether we will forbear. As prophets they wear the mantle once worn by religious figures.

It has been said that prophets are concerned more with insight than with foresight. That is certainly true of scientists. The most important of their insights is their understanding that there can never be any fixed and final body of knowledge. All that we know is tentative, a current hypothesis which may at any time be replaced by a hypothesis which is more satisfactory because it explains phenomena more comprehensively and more simply.

This understanding that all knowledge is tentative is hardly likely to increase confidence in an institution whose creeds are considered inviolable and unalterable. It is true that a creed as a statement can be distinguished from the way the statement is understood, and it is sometimes allowed that understanding can change. It was the claim of an Ampleforth monk, now passed to his rest and his reward, that he believed the doctrines of the Catholic Church in whatever sense they may turn out to be true. It is also allowed, thanks chiefly to John Henry Newman, that the original deposit of a doctrine can develop into forms unimagined at the start, like a caterpillar developing into a butterfly. But the generality of the faithful, and not least many of their pastors, feel suspicious of what they see (no doubt wrongly) as manoeuvres which are too clever by half, and demand a return to what they describe as the old certainties of faith. So a David Jenkins, Bishop of Durham, can be accused of apostasy by those who consider fixity and finality to be the hallmarks of Christian understanding.

The general impression is thus created that the churches claim to possess information which remains for ever valid, and this conflicts with what the scientific method proves empirically not to be the case. Doubts therefore inevitably arise about the truth of what the churches claim as true.

Philosophers of religion may point to the difference between the data on which scientists work and the nature of religious truth. They may point

133

out that the empirical methods of science are suitable for what in principle can be observed, weighed and measured, but that religion is concerned with phenomena of a totally different kind, more like, though not identical with, aesthetic experience. Such arguments doubtless have a great deal of validity, but the man in the street, even if he is educated, can hardly be expected to master subtleties of that kind. The churches appear to offer knowledge of what is the case (does a great picture tell us what is the case?) which is forever settled and unchanging, and science appears to have shown that such knowledge does not exist.

The greatest challenge of science to established religions, therefore, is its demonstration of the tentative nature of all we think we know. Particular beliefs about this or that, where science and religion seem to say different things, are only minor and subsidiary.

Pure science is the pursuit of knowledge for its own sake. But there is also applied science, medicine for example, which can be called technology. Technology seems to make man the master of his own fate. God is superfluous.

In a much-misunderstood statement, Dietrich
Bonhoeffer described man as having come of age.
He did not mean that man had arrived at a state
of moral and emotional maturity. He lived in
Hitler's Germany, and for his opposition to the
Nazis he was imprisoned and subsequently mar-
tyred by them. The condition Germany was in at
that time was hardly conducive to a belief in the
moral progress of mankind. What Bonhoeffer was
referring to was the advancement of technology
which enabled man to be in charge of things
which in the past he could not regulate. Man was
no longer simply the victim of misfortunes like
plague, pestilence and famine. He was grown-up
enough to control and eradicate them by technology, as (after Bonhoeffer's death) smallpox
was eradicated from the face of the earth. And
however long it takes, we are confident that the
same will in time be true of cancer and Aids.

Man's coming of age meant that he no longer
needed a God to put things right. Man could do
it for himself.

If, for instance, there is today an outbreak
of cholera, the appropriate medical steps are
taken and the epidemic brought effectively under

control. When in 1831 cholera reached England
from Europe there were, as Owen Chadwick tells
us, 'cries to close theatres and ballrooms, to
destroy card-tables, to remedy breaches in
keeping the Sabbath, and to end parsons who
hunted'.[5] Parliament petitioned William IV for a
day of fasting and humiliation. Later in the century when there loomed a similar threat, a similar
petition was made by the godly to Lord
Palmerston who, after being a belligerent Foreign
Secretary, was then prime minister. Palmerston
refused the petition, treating Heaven, it was said,
as a foreign power.[6]

It is not enough only that man can now do what
in previous ages it was thought only God could
do; even with things still out of man's control
their antecedents and ultimate causes are scientif-
ically understood so that they are no longer considered as an act of God. Drought and flood are
obvious examples. He would need to be a bold
or insensitive parson who now included in his
service a prayer for rain, for what sends or with-
holds it is now known to depend on climatic con-

[5] Owen Chadwick, *The Victorian Church* (London:
A. & C. Black, 1966–70).
[6] Ibid.

ditions stretching far into the past. We are a long way here from the carefully worded petition in the Book of Common Prayer which asks for 'moderate rain and showers'. Clearly floods had been known to succeed drought.

What scientific knowledge and technology have destroyed is a utilitarian view of God, valued for what he can do rather than for what he is, like a picture which is valued not for its aesthetic qualities but for the money it can fetch in the auction-room. The deepest Christian thinkers, Catholic and Protestant, have always insisted that God must be loved for what he is in himself and not for any benefits he may bestow. So the advance of technology can be seen to provide a necessary and powerful spiritual purgation, as well as fulfilling God's ancient command to man to 'have dominion' – a command understood in the down-to-earth maxim that God helps those who help themselves, or in Cromwell's order to his troops to keep their powder dry. Yet many preachers, out of loyalty to what they believe to be the biblical revelation, still speak of the God who acts in history, without explaining that he acts through the natural and in principle observable uniformities of the created order, including what has and will be discovered about historical causation – what, for instance, caused the French Revolution. If the historian is not a dogmatic determinist he will in the realm of causation find a place for the wills and affections of men and women which, for good or evil, can alter.

Without these qualifications the God who acts in history will look like a magician, and magic is not worship but manipulation. It will not encourage the more thoughtful to come to church, especially when it is seen that the magic does not work.

Science and technology may make God look unnecessary, but only the God considered as the highest and best utility. Pure science, meanwhile, will continue to bear its most important witness that all knowledge is tentative. This will be awkward, as we have seen, for many established religions with their creeds and dogmas founded on the principles that truth lies always in antiquity. If as a result even fewer people go to church, the conclusion can still be drawn that the true God is none the less being truly glorified. For he totally transcends the institutions which claim his sanction or even regard him as a commodity for which they have the patent.

✳   ✳   ✳

Familiarity in our global village with other great religions has made the claim of the Christian churches to be the sole depositories of religious truth look decidedly shaky.

It is interesting to notice how Christian claims have become gradually less sweeping as other religions have become available not simply as objects of inspection but as sources of experience.

In the last century it was confidently assumed that the whole world would be won for Christianity, hopes clustering first around India, and when that failed, with less assurance around China. The assumption was that Christianity was true, the other religions false, and the truth was bound to prevail 'till each remotest nation has learned Messiah's name'.

When things did not work out according to this pattern it was admitted that a serious mistake had been made. It was insensitive to regard the other great religions as wholly false. They had in them elements of truth which demanded to be discerned. Christianity could then be offered to

139

them as the fullness of that truth which they had only partially apprehended. Christian claims were still imperial, but it was a modified imperialism. Sincere attempts to discern elements of truth in other religions involved a willingness to put oneself in the way of experiencing what they had to offer. In order to be understood properly they had not only to be learnt but lived. As learnt in terms of theological ideas and doctrines they were seen to differ, often radically, from Christian belief. But as lived they seemed to deliver spiritual goods remarkably similar to the Christian variety. The question then arose whether attempts at conversion should be continued. If much the same spiritual goods were available to a devout Hindu as to a Christian, what was the point of trying to convert him? So, for example, Simone Weil compared the devout practice of a religion to the craft of a writer in his native language. To persuade a writer to change the language in which he was accustomed to write for another language would most certainly diminish the quality and impact of his writing. And what was true in the realm of language was also true in the realm of religion. Change would involve spiritual diminishment.

How were the Christian churches to react to this probability?

Their whole history made it almost impossible for them totally to renounce their imperial claims. Various manoeuvres were suggested. It had always been part of the Christian orthodoxy that the Eternal Word enlightens every man. Should it therefore, it was asked, be a surprise to discover that the Eternal Word was enlightening devout Hindus and Buddhists? True, they could not after all be recognized as Christians, that is, as Christians without qualification. For their beliefs differed from and often contradicted Christian beliefs, most notably in their failure or refusal to accept that in the historical Jesus Ultimate Reality was made man. How then could a person be described who was not a Christian but whose religion was capable of bearing fruit which decidedly was? Here the idea of anonymity came to the rescue. Devout Hindus and Buddhists could be described as anonymous Christians. They were like a Frenchman who, without realizing it or wanting it, was also a British citizen and who, by refusing a British passport, was thereby not quite qualified to claim one; or like a beggar in a fairy-tale who was a prince in disguise, but who by

141

refusing his royal inheritance was not a prince as princes should be.

Thus to describe the adherents of other religions as anonymous Christians was a makeshift solution intended to preserve the Christian claim of sole possession of the full and final truth. It sat loose to the old scholastic maxim that a thing could not both be and not be at the same time, and it could, obviously, be used against the exclusivism it was designed to protect: were Christians in their turn anonymous Hindus or Buddhists?

Professor John Hick has argued for a Copernican revolution in the Christian estimate of other religions.[7] Christians should abandon their exclusivist claim and ask about a person whether he is ego-orientated or Reality-orientated. In this view, salvation consists of a change from ego-orientation to Reality-orientation. So in the Christian scheme a person can die to his own selfish self and be born again to a life centred on the risen Christ. The same death and rebirth can be found in other religions, albeit in different sets of symbols.

[7]   John Hick, *God Has Many Names* (London: Macmillan, 1980).

By and large, the churches have not taken too kindly to Professor Hick's suggestions. Admittedly they raise problems with which he has not yet had time to deal, especially about the significance in traditional Christianity of the historical Jesus. But Professor Hick can take comfort from the fact that the treatise of Copernicus was put on the Index of forbidden books and remained there for a century and a half!

While this discussion of the relation of Christianity to other religions remained in specialist hands and was for all practical purposes an issue confronted only in far-off lands, it had no general impact. It was the concern of missionaries, theological scholars and a few professional churchmen. Otherwise it was ignored. But as the world grew smaller, with journeys to the Far East becoming only a matter of hours, while immigrants in large numbers arrived in this country from the old empire, the question stared everybody in the face: what were the Christian churches to make of other religions?

It was noticeable that the churches did not try to convert the Muslims, Hindus, Buddhists and Sikhs in their midst, and indeed sometimes

143

offered their redundant places of worship to an immigrant community for the practice of their own religion. (The theological implications of such practical gestures were little less than decisive if only implicit.) Subsequently there arose questions about schooling, with the right of children in school to be taught the faith of their parents and not to be indoctrinated with Christianity. But that is not our concern. What is important for our purposes is that other great religions became available to the people of this country, not even just a few hours' flight away (though quite a number of people took advantage of that) but in the next street – a religion which could not only be looked at from the outside but joined and lived. A monument to this state of affairs can be found in the great gilded figure of the Buddha erected in Battersea Park and consecrated with the chanting of a large crowd of monks in their saffron-coloured robes. Religion had become a matter of consumer choice. For the Christian churches the result was twofold, depending upon a person's disposition.

If he were a sincere seeker after religious truth, he might bypass the Church and find his spiritual needs supplied by, say, a Buddhist centre of contemplation. Theoretically he might then be defined as an atheist, though a perceptive Christian might consider this far from the full truth. Monica Furlong, for instance, wrote to me of a woman she knows well that she is 'a God-filled Buddhist atheist', just as Spinoza with his *Deus sive Natura*, God or Nature, was described by William Temple as a 'God-intoxicated man'. even if in his system there was no place for a God metaphorically out there. In short, the Christian churches have had to reckon with other religions supplying spiritual needs which they themselves have appeared unable to meet.

On the other hand, many people are by disposition non-religious. Their religion consists of ethical endeavour. They try to be good citizens and family-men, and they may work zealously for the promotion of some public good. In former days when the only organized religion was some form of Christianity, they would probably have felt it necessary to ask themselves why they did not go to church and find some answer they considered valid. But the multiplication of religions available has made that a question which is no longer urgent, if it has not led to its disappearance altogether. With a variety of religions on offer, a person

145

may sincerely feel that he is not qualified to choose between them. He is like a person confronted with a number of health-diets, each claiming to be the best or only effective kind, who concludes that he need concern himself with none of them.

The availability of other religions either a few hours away or on the doorstep has been by no means a negligible factor in making the Christian churches seem irrelevant.

* * *

Many volumes have been written about how to reconcile the existence of suffering with a universe allegedly created and constantly held in being by a good and omnipotent God. But these dissertations have carried little weight because they do not provide any convincing answer to the problem. The fact of suffering remains the greatest of all obstacles to belief in the God whom the churches proclaim.

Even the most devout and orthodox of Christians often find it a relief, like the opening of a window in an oppressively stuffy room, when the sense of moral outrage at innocent suffering is expressed without inhibition. Ivan Karamazov's refusal to enter into eternal bliss because the cost of it has been the brutal torture of children is constantly quoted.[8] Christians admire him for returning his ticket even if they lack the resolution to return their own. They may find A.E. Housman's bludgeon 'whatever brute or blackguard made the world' unattractive, but somewhere within them it finds a responsive chord, however deeply repressed it usually is.

By his own home-cut path the average agnostic will often find his way to a position similar to the one argued in a famous essay by Professor Antony Flew,[9] and though it may lack Flew's philosophical clarity and rigour it will be experienced as a feeling no less strong for that. Flew argued that to say God is good is meaningless. It is a statement empty of content because nothing is held to contradict it. When we say that a human person is good, certain conditions have to be met for the statement to be meaningful. If we find

8   Fydor Dostoevsky, *The Brothers Karamzov*, trans. Constance Garnett (London: Heinemann, 1968), p. 252.
9   Antony Flew, *New Essays in Philosophical Theology*, (London: SCM Press, 1963), pp. 96–7.

147

that he has been abominably cruel to his wife and children and has murdered his mistress, then we can no longer call him good. But God is held to be good whatever happens, whether earthquakes kill and maim thousands of people or young children die in agony of cancer. Without any human intervention God has tortured and killed infinitely more people than the worst human tyrant. But he is still said to be good. Nothing, it is held, can count against that claim. Therefore it is gibberish. It is like saying that a traffic light is always green even when it turns amber and red. The description 'green' is thus emptied of meaning. People are not led to this view by following any philosophical fashion. It is the result of costly experience and moral insight.

The old account of why suffering exists no longer holds. God, it was said, created the world perfect, and man spoilt it by his sinful disobedience to God's command. The sin of Adam was inherited by generation after generation, and it was sin which brought suffering as its result. It was not only to us that the sin of Adam was transmitted. It also brought cosmic consequences: 'Cursed is the ground for thy sake' (Gen. 3.17). In short, whatever of suffering there is in the world, it is man's fault, either directly as the result of his own personal sin, or as a result of a sinfulness he has inherited and which has infected his physical environment.

There is no need to say that nobody now holds this view. But no satisfactory alternative explanation has taken its place. The churches can make no moral sense of undeserved suffering, nor do they have any valid suggestion of how the moral score is to be put right. There is sometimes talk of what is called an eschatological solution, that is, of what happens at the end of and beyond the historical process in a supernatural order. But this is only the old heaven which Ivan Karamazov refused.

It should be noticed that his refusal, when he made it, was revolutionary. Christians felt no moral difficulty in accepting the idea of heaven as a more-than-adequate compensation for the injustices of earthly suffering. The books, they thought, would be more than balanced. In this world a person, for no moral rhyme nor reason, might suffer outrageously, but it did not matter as much as it might because all would be made good in the next world. Half a minute of heaven would make 80 years of earthly suffering seem positively

149

joyous. Children might die in great pain of disease, but the Heavenly Jerusalem would be full of laughing boys and girls playing in the streets thereof. This hope was of great practical use. It made suffering easier to endure or contemplate. It acted as both a sedative and a stimulant. When this life was considered as little more than a preparation for eternity, what happened to people on earth remained of only relative importance. It was said of Dr Alington, the headmaster of Eton, that when a parent asked him what was the general purpose of the education the school provided, he answered: 'To prepare boys for the next world.' The answer was no doubt elicited by a certain type of parent, but nobody at the time could have disputed that it was thoroughly Christian.

It is not here being argued that such a conviction is untrue, but that in these days those outside the Church (and many within) cannot in good conscience accept it. For them it smacks too much of the *deus ex machina*, like a fairy-tale in which, after many trials and tribulations, the prince and the princess live happily ever after.

Emphasis among Christian thinkers has thus shifted from heaven to the conviction that God himself suffers in and with his creation – a fact which Christ is believed to have revealed. The view has been well summarized by Charles Williams:

> God made us; He maintained us in our pain. At least, however, on the Christian showing, He consented to be Himself subject to it. If, obscurely, He would not cease to preserve us in the full horror of existence, at least He shared it. He became as helpless as we under the will which is He. This is the first approach to a sense of justice in the whole situation.[10]

Doubtless this line of argument can bring a certain morbid consolation, but there are many, Camus among them, who do not find it morally satisfying. Does equal suffering for all, God included (they ask) make suffering morally acceptable. If an innocent child is in agony, how does it put things right that God himself is also in agony? Does it not rather testify to a moral irresponsibility, like a parent who gives his small child

[10] Charles Williams, *Selected Writings* ed. Anne Ridler (Oxford: Oxford University Press, 1961), p. 95.

fire to play with and is himself badly burnt as he rescues the child from the flames into which he has been allowed to fall? Love might have been wise enough to prevent the accident in the first place. After all, earthquakes and cancer have nothing to do with free will.

Arguments about God and human suffering could be extended almost indefinitely. The purpose of the samples given here is to illustrate how the existence of innocent suffering is the most serious and seemingly insurmountable obstacle to belief in the churches' God.

FIVE

A Wedding Address

It was G.K. Chesterton who said that most probably we are still in Eden. It is only our eyes which have changed. He would, I'm sure, have agreed that sometimes the distorting mirrors fall from our eyes like scales so that for the moment we see things as they really are.

And that is what is happening to us this afternoon as we witness this marriage. Please don't think that I'm insulting the bridal couple by being sentimental at their expense. False feeling and cheap gush have no place in a ceremony of marriage. For when a man and woman surrender themselves to each other what we are confronted with is reality, reality which is glorious because it is stark. For a marriage is not just a matter of social convention, just one of those contrivances which civilized man has thought up to make existence more tidy and property more secure. A marriage is a sacrament of God's real presence with his children because it embodies that self-giving love which is the heart and life-blood of the universe.

What self-giving love involves we see in the Eternal Word made flesh – in the life, death and resurrection of Jesus Christ. In Jesus Christ we see how stark and costly self-giving love must often needs be.

In terms of a marriage there will be in the love of husband and wife, if that love is true, a time to weep as well as a time to laugh, a time to mourn as well as a time to dance, a time to keep silence as well as a time to speak – yes, and there will even be a time to hate as well as a time to love (so that false love may be exposed), a time for war as well as a time for peace.

If there is to be real self-giving, times like that must be both expected and accepted. But they are not the final and ultimate truth. Christ's love for mankind leads him to his cross. But the stark reality of that cross is shown forth for what it most truly and ultimately is on the Mount of Transfiguration where Jesus is revealed in his eternal glory, a glory which nothing in heaven or on earth can take away. And that glory is the most real and ultimate meaning of your life together. Your self-giving love for each other will bring with it a mutual self-fulfilment. In losing your life to each other you will find it in all its unending richness, and you will discover that Christ has given you both his glory as your very own, so that your joy, like his, may be full.

So don't be taken in by the ups and downs which are inevitable in any marriage. They have their own level of reality and mustn't be ignored, and certainly you will need common sense to cope with them. But you must also pray for eyes to see them for what they most truly are on the deepest level of reality: the threads from which is being woven your happiness, your fulfilment, your joy, your glory.

So the words of Jesus on the Mount he addresses to you this afternoon: 'Be not afraid.' For he has called you to find himself, to find his own presence and love in each other. And his love is stronger than anything which seeks to destroy it, stronger even than death itself.

We see you now, therefore, reigning with him in the heavenly places, your deep and intimate human love for each other being the vehicle and vessel of his eternal and unconquerable love. That is why you have opened our eyes today to Paradise regained. We thank God for the vision you are giving us and we pray that you, with us all, may ever be able to perceive it.

Appendix

Harry Abbot Williams
10 May 1919–30 January 2006

Harry Abbot Williams was one of the group of theologians, commonly associated with Cambridge, whose discontent with traditional methods of Christian teaching and preaching found voice among the postwar generation of the 1950s and 60s in a call for a reform more radical than any mere 'restatement' of accepted Christian standards in faith and morals. In this group, never homogeneous enough to acknowledge or formulate a common programme, Williams was perhaps (apart from that 'rogue elephant' Bishop John Robinson) both the most controversial and the most widely influential figure.

* * *

Entering Trinity College, Cambridge, in 1938 from Cranleigh School with a scholarship in history, he was able to remain in residence as a candidate for ordination for the full degree course, taking a first in theology in his third year. He was ordained from Cuddesdon in 1943, and served his first curacies in wartime London at

St Barnabas, Pimlico, and All Saints, Margaret Street. The Catholic atmosphere in which his parochial experience was gained gave a colour to his religious thinking which later reaction never obliterated. Before he left London on his appointment as Chaplain-Tutor at Westcott House, Cambridge, he had already won a reputation as a preacher, and in 1951 he returned to his old college as Lecturer in Theology, later becoming Dean of Chapel and Tutor. Soon after this move came the nervous breakdown which involved him in prolonged courses of analysis and curative treatment, and drove him to an intensive study of Freudian and post-Freudian psychology, which more than anything else determined his critical attitude to traditional Christianity. Between the 1951 Lent book (*Jesus and the Resurrection*) commissioned by the Bishop of London, and the collection of sermons (*The True Wilderness*) of 1965 there is all the distance between spiritual comfort and ruthless challenge – a passage measured by a series of addresses and interviews on radio and television and culminating in the articles and lectures contributed to the volumes *Soundings, The God I Want* and *Objections to Christian Belief.* The constant theme, on which he came to dwell with little variation, was a modern version of the ancient 'Know thyself', coupled with an unqualified repudiation of the (supposed) Christian obsession with sin, self-contempt and self-humiliation. God's forgiveness means that God's love embraces us not as we may become but as we are – and we have to learn to 'accept ourselves because we have been accepted'.

The appeal of this new theology, as might be expected, was felt most by the unsatisfied fringe of thoughtful Christians and fellow-travellers; but the respect in which Williams came to be held by more orthodox churchmen was shown by the welcome extended to him as a member of more than one official or unofficial group formed for the discussion of doctrinal or ecclesiastical questions – including a theological conference in Russia between Anglicans and Orthodox. His observable impact upon the religious thought and practice of academic youth was every bit as much as his notoriety outside the University might have suggested. The sermons (published in 1965 under the title *The True Wilderness*) were hailed by one reviewer as 'a spiritual classic of the twentieth century'. Preached as most of them were in Trinity College chapel, they attracted packed undergraduate congregations. Williams admitted privately in later years that the experience of climbing into a pulpit always terrified him in spite of his huge following.

It is likely that his personal influence both upon his tutorial pupils and upon the younger Fellows of the college, who would seldom hear him preach, was more ultimately significant.

In 1969 Williams decided to retire from academic life and join the Anglican religious community at Mirfield in Yorkshire, known as The Community of the Resurrection. The community had been founded by Charles Gore and among its outstandingly gifted members over the years had been Raymond Raynes, Trevor Huddleston and Geoffrey Beaumont. A recruit with Williams' outstanding intellectual gifts was a prized addition to the community, and he was treated as such without having to undergo the full rigours of monastic discipline. This was probably not good for him; certainly it was not good for the community.

Shortly after taking solemn vows he published a small masterpiece called *The Joy of God* (1979), followed in 1982 by his autobiography *Some Day I'll Find You*. This showed much of the genius of his spirit and his abounding sense of humour, though many found the text a little snobbish and tired of the accounts of his friendship with the titled and the famous.

Thereafter, his literary output ceased and he embarked on 24 years of self-communion in the monastery – punctuated by frequent outings to Chatsworth and London, where his great friend John Betjeman put his Chelsea house at Williams' disposal.

It was soon after the publication of *The True Wilderness* in 1965 (still in print today and selling vigorously) that Williams made it clear that his orientation was homosexual. This gave him a particular perception into human nature and the pastoral care he gave to his pupils and former pupils was exceptional. At Trinity one of his pupils was involved in a near-fatal car accident and was unconscious for some time. Williams got to his knees and prayed his heart out. The result was positive and the young man recovered.

From Mirfield he was occasionally tempted out to preach and his sermons remained outstanding. In 1976 for example he preached at the wedding of a former pupil in a Catholic church and showed a profound understanding of the nature of marriage and Christian marriage such that most heterosexual priests would be incapable of. There is a lesson here for those contemporary Anglican bishops who wish to extirpate homosexual clergy from their dioceses.

* * *

It would be an incomplete obituary of Harry Williams that did not mention his friendship with the Prince of Wales, who came to Trinity College, Cambridge, as an undergraduate in 1966. The Prince called his son Harry, and long after Williams entered the monastery, he would call Mirfield to seek Harry Williams's advice and wise counsel. Williams took part in the marriage service of Prince Charles to Lady Diana Spencer.

* * *

Along with Michael Ramsey, Alan Ecclestone, W.H. Vanstone and Rowan Williams, Harry Williams was one of the very few outstanding Anglican theologians of the postwar years.

Robin Baird-Smith